Seeking New Possibilities?
Be a Search Consultant!

Terre Davis, PhD

Library of Congress Control Number: 2010900696
ISBN: Hardcover   978-1-4500-3102-8
               Softcover   978-1-4500-3101-1
               Ebook   978-1-4500-3103-5

This book was printed in the United States of America.

To order additional copies of this book, contact:
Xlibris Corporation
1-888-795-4274
www.Xlibris.com
Orders@Xlibris.com
70654

Dedicated to my husband and best friend,
Dr. Tom Davis. Your unwavering support and never ending
encouragement is a real treasure.

Acknowledgements

Many thanks to the first Board of Education who hired me as its search consultant and to all Board Members who have dedicated countless hours in seeking the very best leader for the school community in which they serve.

Contents

Book Preface

Experiencing the process of interviewing for a school superintendent position was challenging, to say the least. In my experience, I was appalled by the lack of professionalism and organization shown on the part of the school districts. I made notes of how I thought the interview process should be conducted and put my notes away, thinking that someday I might want to do something regarding the professional interview process.

Upon retirement from serving as a public school superintendent for nearly twelve years, I referred to the notes I had made during the interview process and determined that there was a need in this professional arena. I did research and then started my own company for the purpose of doing superintendent searches with boards of education. I have completed over one hundred individual searches and feel that I have developed and perfected a process that is second to none. I have decided that I need to share the information and experiences I have gained so that others may benefit through my process.

I feel that in the very near future, many boards of education are not going to have the funds to hire a consultant to assist them in a superintendent search; therefore, I would like to make available a search process which has been very successful for the past twenty-plus years.

The decision in hiring a new superintendent is the most important decision a board will ever make; therefore, the process to get to the right decision is extremely important. Many boards think it is just a simple matter and try to do it on their own without specific guidelines. *What a mistake!*

This book is a step-by-step method with all materials suited to the specific needs of the district, whether a small, rural, large, urban, charter, or private school. Here, the author also discusses the materials as valuable and appropriate in searching for a college dean or working with a private company.

This book would be extremely valuable to, and is intended for, boards of education, any corporation, or any other organization in the public or private sector seeking a process for hiring the next superintendent, university dean, or corporate CEO, and as a textbook or reference material for university graduate studies.

While searching for publications of a similar nature, I have found this book to be unique and have no rival.

Chapter One

HOW TO GET YOUR BUSINESS STARTED

1. NAME YOUR BUSINESS.

You may want to use your own name such as, "Bob Jones, Search Consultant" or "Bob Jones and Associates, Search Consultants", or "BJ and Associates", etc.

2. REGISTER YOUR BUSINESS.

Register your business with the local registration office and acquire a Federal Identification Number. This step is crucial as you are an "independent contractor" with boards of education.

3. DEVELOP PROMOTIONAL MATERIALS.

Have business cards and letterhead stationery designed and printed.

4. DEVELOP A CONTACT LIST.

Inform several organizations and persons that you are starting your own business. Some of them will certainly be your competitors. This task could be done by personal visits to offices, businesses, or through the mail, as examples.

5. DETERMINE YOUR COST OF DOING BUSINESS.

Do research of competitive costs, determine your baseline cost plus expenses, as this amount will need to be listed in your contract with the board of education.

6. DEVELOP A CONTRACT.

A sample contract is provided (A). The contract outlines the proposal. However, contact your own legal advisor regarding your particular needs.

7. DEVELOP A PROPOSAL TO PRESENT TO BOARDS OF EDUCATION.

A written proposal outlining your tasks to a board of education must be ready to be presented when requested. Included with the proposal should be an introductory letter, along with any additional promotional materials you may want to include, such as a written guarantee. Samples of the letter (B), proposal (C) and guarantee (D) are included in the reference list.

8. BE READY FOR THE INTERVIEW.

When you are requested to interview with a board of education, do your homework (know something about the district and board members, etc.), be organized, and be ready! Know how much time you have for your presentation, and stick to it!

9. YOU HAVE LANDED THE JOB!

Get your contract signed and follow the step-by-step procedure.

Now that you have all of the above tasks completed, you are ready to begin. Following the step-by-step procedures provided, you should find great success in your "new" career!

Chapter Two

GETTING STARTED

Selecting a new superintendent is one of the most important decisions a school board will ever have to make. Decisions regarding the process to select a new superintendent become paramount to ensure that the task is completed in an efficient and professional manner. The following information must be known by the search consultant before he/she starts the search process. The information may also be used in assisting the board of education to determine which process is best for its particular needs.

FACTORS THAT INFLUENCE THE SEARCH PROCESS:

1. DEPARTURE OF CURRENT SUPERINTENDENT

    a. Retirement
    Usually an expected event, the superintendent gives notice—plenty of time for the board to decide which course of action to take, such as hiring an inside person or doing a search. The board should not expect the current superintendent to have any involvement in, or influence upon, the employment of his/her successor. Hiring a superintendent is the board's responsibility, and it must live with the decision it makes. If the current superintendent is involved in any way, he/she may become the lightning rod for anything negative which could happen with the new superintendent.

    b. Another position
    This event may occur suddenly, depending upon the current superintendent's contract with the current board. If the departure is sudden, the board must decide if it will employ an internal person or an outsider as the "interim" superintendent. If an insider is appointed, it must be made very clear to the insider, himself/herself, and all others that the insider is *not* a candidate for the permanent superintendent position. If an outsider is considered to be the interim, usually a retired superintendent is a great asset to the board as he/she has a track record as a superintendent and

is able to step in without a lot of lost time or needed guidance. The board should *not* use the interim to guide the search.

c. Forced departure—many reasons such as illegal acts, individual board members' attitudes, pressure groups (unions, boosters, community, political, individuals, etc)

This is probably the most disruptive form of departure for all persons involved. The board members may be split in the decision to dismiss the superintendent. Employees, community members, students, political influences, etc., may all become a part of the action. Leadership must come from the board in determining the necessary steps to return the district to a place of teaching and learning. There are no easy answers to this dilemma and depending upon the nature of the departure, it may take several months to fully recover and the community will never forget.

d. Unfortunate—sickness, death, family, etc.

The shock is emotional for all persons involved, and an immediate decision regarding an interim is mandatory. An internal person or a former superintendent known to the district would be the most responsible decision. Again, the board should follow the guideline that neither of the above-mentioned persons would be a candidate for the permanent position.

2. THE SEARCH—NECESSARY OR UNNECESSARY

Whatever the circumstances are regarding the current superintendent's departure, the board must decide if it is interested in hiring an internal candidate. There are pros and cons to this decision, and the first factor to be determined is whether or not an internal candidate is available. Many districts now attempt to "grow their own" and will have a person ready to appoint to the position. This often happens when the current superintendent is retiring. The transition is smooth and any major dissention is unlikely.

However, if the board is *not* unanimous in appointing an internal candidate who has made his/her candidacy known, then the board has several options:

1) Hire the internal candidate on a one-year contract with a decision on whether to make the person permanent within the first eight months of the contract. If the decision is to make the person permanent, then stability sets in, if not, then the board has time to do a search.
2) Launch a search, and state that all internal candidates are encouraged to apply. However, if external candidates know that there is an internal candidate, many will decide not to apply as they feel that the internal candidate will likely be appointed.

3) If there is more than one internal candidate, the board should either interview all internal candidates first and make a decision, or launch a search and encourage all internal candidates to apply. Again, if external candidates know that there are internal candidates, many may choose not to apply as they may feel that the board will appoint an internal candidate.

3. INTERNAL CANDIDATES

When a board has a single internal or "homegrown" candidate (who has made his/her desire to become the next superintendent well-known) and it determines to do a search instead of appointing the internal person, several results may become apparent:

1. The board is not unanimous in appointing the inside candidate.
2. The board feels that it has a "duty" to search the field (makes the board look good to the community, that the board is doing its job).
3. Tells the internal candidate that he/she is apparently not good enough to be appointed
4. Sends a clear message to all future internal candidates that they need not to strive to be "home-grown"
5. The pool of candidates will not be as large as many candidates will know that there is an internal candidate.

Pros of an internal candidate:

1. The time for transition from current superintendent to the new superintendent is minimal and generally smooth.
2. There is barely a "blip" on the screen as the new superintendent is able to hit the ground running and continue on with activities and goals of the district.
3. Already knows where the "warts" are
4. Knows employees and stakeholders
5. Knows the board of education
6. Has external connections already in place with education, business, and industry
7. Lends stability to the district
8. Is politically astute—knows the internal and external politics within the district
9. Has a track record within the district

Cons of an internal candidate:

1. Knows too much
2. Knows where the "warts" are
3. Hard to make decisions without involving personalities
4. Has past loyalties and liabilities with parents, students, employees; individual and group pressure, such as booster groups, etc.
5. Leadership style is known, is predictable
6. Can become too comfortable, creativity may be stymied because of known personalities, material limitations, etc.
7. May have difficulties with former peers in the district as now he/she is the boss

4. EXTERNAL CANDIDATES

Advantages of an external candidate:

1. Sees all the trees in the forest
2. No individual or group pressure built in
3. All persons seen as equals, no built-in loyalties
4. Gives a "fresh look" to all aspects of the system
5. Has total board support
6. Able to evaluate programs and situations and make necessary changes with minimal conflicts
7. Make own observations without prior influences

Disadvantages of external candidate:

1. Unknown, no local track record
2. Takes time for the transition
3. Takes more time to evaluate situations, programs, etc., in order to make decisions

SEARCH PROCESS PROCEDURES

Once the board has determined to launch the search process, it must decide if it is going to hire a search consultant or do the entire process on its own.

1. BOARD DRIVEN, DOING THE SEARCH ON ITS OWN

If the board determines to launch the process on its own, there needs to be someone to lead the charge. The person in charge should *not* be an employee or a board member due to his/her "ties" to the school district but rather, someone from the community who is respected and trusted by the board and the community as a whole (perhaps a past board member). The chairperson could use the guidelines provided in this book to carry out the entire search process.

Advantages:

1. Less costly
2. Gives a sense of "community success, we did it ourselves"

Disadvantages:

1. More time-consuming
2. Possibility of making unfortunate mistakes
3. Difficulty in keeping total confidentiality regarding candidates
4. Input (focus) groups may not be as open and honest when sharing their thoughts and ideas as the chairperson is also a stakeholder
5. May have to deal with individual/group pressure
6. Too many people may want to make the "decision"

2. HIRING A SEARCH CONSULTANT

If the board determines to hire a search consultant, it should interview firms that provide this service in order to determine which firm it feels would meet its needs and has personnel who would work well with the board. There are specific questions that boards should ask all firms to determine the firm's experience, knowledge, success rate and openness to *all* candidates. (Ref. #1)

Advantages:

1. Has no ties to community
2. Has a track record of success
3. Provides guidance to board and community
4. Knows many candidates
5. Has many connections outside of the district
6. Provides specific guidelines and suggested legal documents regarding the search

Disadvantages:

1. More costly
2. Less personalized

Chapter Three

LAUNCHING THE SEARCH PROCESS

SETTING SEARCH GUIDELINES:

1. Calendar

The board should adopt a calendar (Ref. #2) for the search process from the beginning of the process to the signing of the contract and the date the new superintendent is to start. The entire process should take no more than ten weeks. If the process extends more than ten weeks, persons involved become complacent, and the issue is no longer on the "front burner". Also, candidates who are searching for a new position may withdraw to accept another position as they don't want to "wait".

2. Educational requirements

The board should adopt the desired educational requirements it wants in the new superintendent, such as NCA (North Central Association) qualifications, doctorate degree, administrative experience, etc. It is wise to list the educational requirements as "preferred" requirements for the reason that someone who is close to meeting a specific requirement may then apply, whereas if specific requirements are mandatory, the candidate may not and should not apply.

3. Base salary

A base salary should be established, as it would provide the candidate with information to assist him/her in making the decision to apply. A candidate needs to determine if he/she could afford to leave his/her current position. Some boards think they should offer a salary range, which has a disadvantage, as all candidates would expect the uppermost range. Listing a salary as "competitive" means nothing as candidates question the salary as competitive to what? This area often causes difficulty in contract negotiations.

A base salary could be determined through various means. However, the most simple and fair way is to gather information from districts in the same athletic league, same geographical area, and those of similar size. I suggest that the superintendent or business manager in each district suggested above be contacted personally to obtain the information regarding the current yearly base salary and amount of a board paid annuity for the superintendent. Many times, surveys which are published are incorrect. All other benefits are varied to such a degree, that an average or comparison is nearly impossible. After obtaining the base salary and board paid annuity amount of each superintendent, one should then add the two numbers for the total base salary paid to the superintendent in each district. All numbers should then be added to determine the average salary without a board-paid annuity and the average salary paid with a board-paid annuity. The board may then determine what salary they want to offer. One must remember that the base salary to be determined is for the next school year and information gathered is for the current school year. (Ref. #3)

4. Number of years of the contract
    A three-year-term contract is normal and fair as candidates do not want the expense and uncertainty of moving to a new job and community for a one—or a two-year contract. A three-year-term contract should be just that, which means the board must renew or terminate the contract within a certain specified timeline as indicated in the superintendent's contract. Some boards become involved in an "evergreen" contract, which means that if the board does not take specific action, the contract is continuous (rolls over every year). Boards have the responsibility to evaluate the superintendent each and every year and make a decision regarding the superintendent's continued employment.
    The above four items—expected date of employment, educational requirements, base salary, and number of years should all be listed in the postings/advertisements.

POSTING THE POSITION

The official posting (Ref. #4) of the position needs to be approved by the board

1. Internal: usually required by all district employee contracts
2. Local area: geographically
3. State: throughout the specific state only
4. Regional: determined by east, midwest, southern, western, etc.
5. National: covers internal, local, state, and the nation as a whole. There are specific organizations one should contact for posting the position. (Ref. #5)

Chapter Four

REQUESTING INPUT/IDEAS/OPINIONS
INPUT/FOCUS GROUPS

The input/focus groups (Ref. #6) provide valuable information for the board to determine which characteristics, leadership skills, and personality traits it would like to see in the new superintendent.

Employee groups should be scheduled for input on their own "turf". Persons are much more likely to be willing to give input if the facilitator holds the meeting at their workplace instead of asking them to meet the facilitator at another meeting place. (Ref. #7)

Employee groups of like positions should meet in groups—elementary teachers meet with their own building peers, custodians meet as a group, building secretaries meet as a group, etc. Reason for this is that groups feel comfortable sharing ideas and thoughts with their own peers.

Letters should be sent out to all employees (Ref. #8) and a news release to citizens. (Ref. #9) The letter should be authored by the board president.

PROCEDURE FOR DOCUMENTING INPUT

The facilitator should write all thoughts and ideas, as they are given, on an easel in front of the specific group. This procedure allows the contributor to see how the facilitator is interpreting what he/she is saying. *All* employee and student group comments are anonymous and known only to those persons in the specific group. The community groups—one scheduled for an afternoon session, one for an evening session, and one for a morning session—are open to all persons in the community, including the press. Depending upon specific state laws, the input session with board members only may or may not be open to the public.

When obtaining impromptu comments from individuals on the street, in stores, etc., the facilitator should write the comment down on a legal pad and then read it back to the contributor so that the contributor can verify what is written is what he/she actually said or meant to say. This signifies to the contributor that his/her comments are valued and appreciated.

USE OF INPUT INFORMATION

When all input sessions are completed, all comments are then placed in a frequency list, which indicates the number of times each comment, or one similar, was contributed. Specific categories are then defined into ten to twelve paragraphs with specific themes such as public relations, curriculum knowledge, etc. All themes are supported by all comments received. That document then becomes the proposed "profile" listing—the characteristics, leadership skills, and personality traits the board is looking for in its new superintendent.

During the entire input group process, the facilitator must be very careful to ensure that the sessions do not become negative and serve as a "vent of the past" for some persons but rather a positive session expressing "what our needs are now, and for the future".

The facilitator provides the listing of all comments (all anonymous and not one group weighing more than another) (Ref. #10), the frequency list (Ref. #11), and the proposed profile (Ref. #12) for board members to review before a meeting in public, at which time, all documentation becomes public. (Even if the state law allows the board to review this information in private, I suggest it be done in public so the contributors are able to see just how their individual comments are valued and appreciated. There is nothing worse than asking someone for input and then not use, value, or appreciate their ideas). The facilitator reviews all information at the board meeting and after discussion and any suggested changes, the board adopts the "profile" which is published for all to see.

Once the profile is adopted by the board of education, a thank-you letter should be sent to employees and citizens. (Ref. #13)

The candidate finds the profile very helpful in determining if he/she "fits" the needs of the district as outlined in the profile.

The process of obtaining input from a community, student, and employee groups, as well as individuals on the street or in stores, is an outstanding public relations tool for the board of education. People like to have someone ask for their opinions, especially if it is in an area which directly affects them. They also like the idea that, in most cases, their opinion is anonymous and that they know the board will **hear** what they had to say. I have found that talking with people on the street, in stores, restaurants, etc., through an impromptu method, gets otherwise uninvolved persons involved in the school district. After all, the schools are owned by the taxpayers and they like the idea that they are being asked for input regarding their investment and for the next leader of the school district.

In over a hundred searches, I have not found any district which has the same exact profile. Of course, some areas are quite similar, but each district has its own specific wants and needs.

The profile process is the best evaluation/input tool the board has in determining its future needs/goals.

Chapter Five

APPLICATIONS

"APPLICANT" VS. "CANDIDATE"

As applicants send in the necessary information requested on the posting (letter of application, completed official application form, current resume, current letters of recommendation, and the names of three persons who will serve as references and can be contacted), the consultant must determine if the individual has completed his/her file. If the applicant has not completed his/her file, the consultant must contact him/her and request the necessary materials. All applicants for the position should be able to follow directions and answer requests for materials as needed. If an applicant does not fulfill a specific request after two attempts by the consultant, the file should be considered incomplete. At this point, the definition of applicant and candidate becomes clear. An "applicant" is a person who has made an attempt to apply for the position but has not completed his/her file as requested. A "candidate" is a person who has completed and filed all of the requested materials. It is important to distinguish the difference, as the numbers of applicants will tend to be very different (higher) than the numbers of candidates (lower). Consultants often report only the number of applicants or call everyone a candidate, which is misleading to all audiences.

FACTORS CONTRIBUTING TO A FEWER NUMBER OF CANDIDATES

Many times consultants and persons quoted in the media will give the opinion that there aren't very many good candidates available. This is an unnecessary, negative statement. Of course, we don't have the number of sixty to seventy-five applicants we had ten to fifteen years ago, but we do have outstanding persons applying for the top jobs in school districts, and they should not have to be lumped into the category of "poor applicants". After all, only one person is going to be hired and no one should be negative when there are at least fifteen to thirty persons from whom to choose. I sometimes think that persons don't apply for a certain position as they don't want to be labeled as "poor".

There are several reasons for the decline in the number of applicants for superintendent positions:

1. Time commitment/family

The superintendent position requires a vast amount of time on the job, not only on the regular ten hours per day basis, but many evening and early morning hours, as well as weekend activities. If the applicant has a family, the time commitment required for the position must be understood and approved by family members. The energy and enthusiasm for the position is also extremely important. An applicant may, and should, research the necessary requirements in this area and determine if he/she wants to make such a time commitment.

In this same area of concern, the board may expect him/her to move into the district. Moving into the school district may discourage/prohibit a person from applying. The decision to move into the district may involve the financial liability of buying and selling a home. Determining the culture of the new district and whether the family will be happy living there is also a concern. If children are involved, it must be determined if the move will be beneficial to each family member. All of the above areas must be thoroughly researched and decisions must be made prior to the formal application.

2. Stress

The stress involved in the superintendent position is difficult to measure. Some persons enjoy the stress and work well with it. Every avenue of the position is as stressful as the person allows it to be, from an unhappy parent to a major budget crisis, etc. Only the applicant can determine if he/she will be able to handle the many and various situations causing him/her stress.

3. Salary and Benefits

Depending upon the geographical area, persons desiring to become a superintendent may take a salary and benefit decrease to become a superintendent. This may occur even if the person is currently in a subordinate position to a superintendent, such as a building principal or assistant superintendent. This is an area of concern to most applicants, given the financial liabilities the applicant has to fulfill. The applicant needs to determine what the minimum level of pay and benefits he/she must have and research the pay and benefits the position is offering or is able to offer. The applicant should research this matter by finding out what the current superintendent is making and what the position is offering in the posting. Research should be done before the applicant applies instead of waiting to determine if he/she can negotiate a satisfactory salary and benefits package once the position is offered, especially if his/her needs appear to be much more than the geographical area will bear.

4. Board of Education

This area may well be the major reason we have seen a decline in the number of applicants. The wise applicant will research the reason why the current superintendent is leaving or has left the position. If the departure has been controversial in any way, applicants need to determine the "why" of the situation. Research regarding board members' attitudes, philosophies, commitment, and professionalism are extremely important. Often when the applicant finds a split board, a micromanaging board, a board president or other member who thinks he/she is the superintendent, or a disrespectful board (to each other or the superintendent), the applicant will not apply, which is certainly understandable.

5. Internal/External Situations

If the budget, curriculum, employee unrest (unions), etc., have a negative perception in the community, or a booster club or public opinion of the district is negative, many applicants will determine that they do not want to tackle a situation which appears negative at the very start of his/her new position. However, another candidate may enjoy taking a position where he/she will be able to start a healing process and make a real difference in the district.

Another reason for applicants to avoid applying for a superintendent position is that he/she may be following a long-term superintendent who was very well liked and was extremely successful. An applicant may feel that he/she will not be able to fill the shoes and may not be able, or encouraged to, apply his or her own talents to the position. "We have always done it this way" may be the overriding theme in the district.

Chapter Six

SCREENING APPLICATIONS

BOARD'S ROLE

As applicants submit their materials as requested, the consultant screens the paperwork to determine if the applicant has met all stated requirements in the posting and to what degree the applicant meets the adopted profile which states the specific needs of the position as determined by the stakeholders. All files remain confidential as candidates are requested to sign a letter indicating so. (Ref. #14). The consultant, upon completion of the posting time frame, should submit all files to the board for each member to do his or her own screening. No file should be copied, as board members should see all of the original materials in the form in which they were submitted. Along with the files, each board member should receive an individual packet containing the following:

1. Guidelines for screening candidate files—important as most board of education members have no idea how to proceed (Ref. #15)
2. An overall profile of the candidates indicating their name, position, current location (city and state), educational degrees, and if all guidelines were met/not met (Ref. #16)
3. Agenda for next meeting (Ref. #17)
4. Letter regarding confidentiality of candidate name, materials, etc. (Ref. #18)
5. List of suggested questions to be used at the interview. (Reference #19) All questions should be crossed referenced with the adopted profile. (Ref. #20) The profile states what the needs are, so we must be certain that the questions reflect the needs.
6. Guide for board members to "score" or make notes regarding candidates. (Ref. #21)
7. Board members should have three to five days in which they may do their own screening.

At this point, the board members do not know which candidates are going to be recommended by the consultant. The reason for this is that each and every candidate should have an equal opportunity to be screened by individual board members. (An exception to this may be if a board member has limited time to review the files and wants to know the list of the top ten to twelve candidates. Even then, it is not a good idea). If the consultant gives a list of only six to eight candidates, then the rest of the candidates would not receive a fair chance to be reviewed by the board members. Many consultants will give only the short list to the board. This practice has been fondly referred to as the "Good Old Boys Club". There are consultants in the profession who will have a list of persons to whom they have promised jobs and will push their candidacy. Some even provide weekend seminars for a hefty fee, and in return, the participants will appear on the consultant's "short list". Moreover, if the candidate hasn't participated in the consultant's seminar and he/she applies for a position which the consultant has posted, no matter how good the candidate is, he/she may not be promoted for an interview. Many candidates become wise to this practice and don't even apply for positions posted by this type of consultant.

CONSULTANT'S ROLE

Upon completion of a candidate's file, and if the candidate meets the board's adopted qualifications and the profile, the consultant should schedule an hour conversation with the candidate, preferably in a face-to-face meeting. However, if that is not possible, a phone conversation is a must. This activity is required for the following reasons:

1. Validate what is in the file. Ask the individual candidate various questions about materials in his/her file; determine if "he/she is who/what he/she says he/she is" (sometimes the candidate doesn't even know what is in his/her file as someone else has completed it and sent it)
2. Determine if the candidate meets the profile
3. Face-to-face conversation assists the consultant in determining the candidate's type of personality
4. Gain more information by asking the list of twenty questions (Ref. #22) of each candidate
5. Determine if the candidate has done his/her homework on the district, his/her interest in the district, commitment to the position, etc.
6. Listen for candidate's priorities in obtaining the position, such as commitment to students, salary and benefits package, etc.
7. Ask candidate if he/she would accept the position for the salary and benefits as stated in the posting.
8. Ask candidate if he/she is a current candidate in any other searches at the present time, and if so, what his/her status is in each search. This will provide important information regarding timelines for the consultant.

The consultant must take copious notes during the meeting with the candidate, as well as the information obtained while calling candidate references in at least two previous positions the candidate has held. The notes taken by the consultant will be shared with the board members during the closed meeting. The board may go into a closed meeting, determined by the candidate's request of confidentiality. State law determines if a closed meeting is legal—for example, in some states, a vote of at least 5-2 of a seven-member board allows the board to go into a closed session. A vote of 4-3 does not allow the board to go into a closed session. Also, if a candidate refused to sign the request for confidentiality form, then the board must discuss this person's candidacy in open session and his/her complete file will become a part of the board minutes. His/her name will be made public, even if the person is not selected to be interviewed.

Chapter Seven

SELECTION OF CANDIDATES TO INTERVIEW

During closed session, only the board members and the consultant are in attendance. At that time, the consultant and board members will share their notes on each candidate. The consultant will go down the list of candidates in alphabetical order and indicate, in the consultant's view, why the candidate should or should not be recommended for an interview. The consultant will share all information received during the one-hour conversation with the candidate and also share all the information received when checking references on each candidate. A discussion between the board members and consultant regarding each candidate takes place. After the session is completed and all thoughts and ideas are shared regarding each candidate, the board returns to open session (determined by state laws) and by motion and vote, determines which candidates (one at a time) are to be interviewed.

All candidates who were given a one-hour session with the consultant should be immediately called and informed of his/her status as a candidate before the press/media releases the names of those candidates who are to be interviewed. Candidates should be given the courtesy of a personal call rather than reading the results of his/her candidacy in the newspaper or hearing it on the late night news. A letter of thanks should be sent to all candidates not receiving an interview. (Ref. #23)

If a candidate was not chosen to be interviewed, he/she is eliminated as a candidate for the position. The names and files of the persons to be interviewed are then made public as determined by state law. The candidates are scheduled for the interview times (dates) as previously approved by the board in the adopted calendar. If the board interviews four to six candidates, an average number, then usually two interviews are held in one evening. Any changes to the calendar at this point must be voted upon.

The day following the decision as to which persons are to be interviewed, the consultant should send a letter to all employees and also provide a press release indicating the candidates' names, current position which includes school district, city, and state, the date, time, and place of the interview. The letter/press release should also invite everyone to attend the interviews and indicate that anyone who may wish to go on the site visit to the final candidates' workplace with the board of education members, must indicate his/her desire to do so by placing it in writing and sending it to the board of education president by the time and place indicated on the letter. It must also state that anyone desiring to attend the site visit(s) must attend *all* of the interviews. (Ref. # 24)

As soon as the names of the candidates to be interviewed are announced, the employee groups may contact their peers in the candidate's district. Hopefully, if anyone obtains negative information, he/she will contact the consultant who may have a solution to the situation, or will pursue the concern to obtain an answer.

Chapter Eight

INTERVIEW PROCEDURES

Once the candidate interviews have been scheduled, the consultant then gives the board a workshop regarding the interview process. (Ref. # 25). Discussion of the do's and don'ts and logistics of the interview take place. All the questions, which were included with the board member packets when they received the candidate files, are reviewed. The consultant should give examples of good answers, bad answers, and around-the-question answers. (Ref. #26) Each question is assigned to a specific board member to be asked of each candidate as each candidate must be asked each question in the same manner. (Ref. #27) Board members are provided a set of questions for each candidate on which the board members may make their own individual notations during the interview. Each board member will also be provided a rating sheet, for the board member's use only, which correlates with each question asked of the candidate. (Ref. #28)

The candidates must be treated equally; therefore, the interviews are scheduled for exactly one hour and fifteen minutes. This assists the board in determining how well the candidate thinks while giving his/her answers. The board president has the responsibility to keep the interview timeline. (Ref. #29) All information regarding the timeline is reviewed with all board members. The timeline is indicated on the list of questions to assist the board members. (Ref. #27)

The consultant also gives examples of what to look for regarding the individual candidate such as individual eye contact with board members, the handshake, nervousness, dress, appearance, etc.

The consultant should also review illegal and inappropriate questions, which should not be asked of any candidate. (Ref. #29)

When the interview workshop session is over, the board members will feel comfortable with the interview process.

The consultant will provide each board member with a copy of each candidate's individual file, prior to the interview. One copy will also be provided in the superintendent's office for anyone to review.

CANDIDATE VISIT TO THE DISTRICT

All candidates who are to be interviewed are encouraged to visit the district prior to the interview with the board. The candidate is given written procedures to follow regarding the visit and the interview with the board. (Ref. #30) The candidate's visit to the district is set up with a designated person in the district administrative office for the candidate to contact. The candidate may wish to visit with the current superintendent, discuss the curriculum, discuss and view budget, visit with the tech director, etc. He/she may also wish to take a tour of the district, visit schools, visit places of business, etc. The candidate may talk with anyone, except board of education members. This is an important time for the candidate to discover everything he/she can about the district. The visit will assist the candidate in determining if he/she is a good fit for the district and if the district is a good fit for him/her.

THE INTERVIEW

All candidates are requested to arrive fifteen minutes before the start of the interview for the purpose of meeting all persons in the audience and the individual board members prior to the start of the interview. This activity helps to relieve some tension when the interview begins and gives board members the opportunity to observe how the candidate reacts in a situation where most persons are strangers to him/her.

The consultant should make sure that the spouse and immediate family are all invited to attend the interview. This will assist the candidate in determining if the position is a good fit for him/her and any family members involved. The family members attending the interview may sit anywhere they desire in the audience area. Attendance of the spouse/family also indicates that the spouse/family is interested and supportive of the candidate.

The interviews should be videotaped. The candidate will be informed of this activity prior to the interview. After the new superintendent has been appointed, all persons who were interviewed will receive the videotape of his/her interview which provides the candidate with a valuable professional development tool and a nice thank-you from the district. The interview setup should include the board members at a table setup in a horseshoe design with the candidate at the open portion of the horseshoe. This allows the candidate to make easy eye contact with all board members. The video camera should be positioned behind the board president and focused directly on the candidate. Monitors should be positioned behind the candidate for all members in the audience who are sitting behind the candidate to see the candidate's face during the interview. This setup promotes the candidate's ability to focus on the board members only and not worry about what is happening in the audience. (Ref. #31) The board president will indicate, at the beginning of the interview, that the total interview will last for one hour and fifteen minutes during which time there are thirty (more or less) questions from the board, questions from the audience, and a closing statement from the candidate. The board president will also indicate to the audience that if anyone wants to ask the candidate a question, he/she should write that question on a three-by-five card, available at the back of the room, and the consultant will collect those questions near the end of the interview. The consultant reviews the written question as it is given to him/her and determines if it is a legal question. If it is not, the consultant will indicate such to the writer and will assist the writer in making it a legal question. The consultant will then take all written questions to the board president who will determine which and how many questions will be asked, depending upon the time remaining.

When the interview concludes, the candidate may stay in the area during the fifteen minutes between the interviews to meet other persons in the audience, answer additional individual questions, and meet the next candidate. When it is time for the candidate to leave, the consultant walks him/her to the door and then asks the candidate if he/she is still a candidate. The interview is a two-way interview. The candidate is being interviewed, but he/she is also interviewing the board. After the opportunity of visiting the district and meeting with the board, if the candidate feels that the job is not a good fit for him/her, then he/she should withdraw at that time and not wait until he/she is selected for a site visit.

Chapter Nine

SELECTION OF FINALISTS

Upon the conclusion of the interviews, the board should take a thirty—to forty-five-minute recess. During this time, the board members may talk with persons in the audience and fellow board members regarding thoughts on which candidates are the best fit for the district and will meet the specific needs of the district as outlined in the profile.

After the recess is concluded, the board returns to session, and the consultant conducts the meeting. (Ref. #32)

The board members have their individual notes from the interview sessions, their comments from persons in the audience, and comments from fellow board members to use in assisting them in making a decision.

The consultant gives the following directions:

We will go around the board table and ask each board member for the strengths of each candidate, one candidate at a time, in the order in which the candidate was interviewed. Board members need not repeat what another has said but may add to previous comments. Then the audience has a chance to add comments on the candidate's strengths to the board members' comments.

We will then return to the board members, starting with the next board member (each board member has at least two times to be the first to comment) and ask, "What would you like to know more about this candidate?" If the board member is *not* interested in continuing this person's candidacy, then the board member says, "I have no further questions". That is an indication that the candidate may be dropped from the final list. A notation is made by the consultant to all contributors that there are to be only positive comments said about any one candidate. No single derogatory comment will be allowed as we want every candidate to remember his/her experience in the district as a positive one, not one of a negative nature just because negative comments were made about him/her in public. We continue around the board table, and if five board members out of the seven total members, are no longer interested by answering "I have no further questions", then the candidate is dropped from further consideration and the audience is not asked for any additional comments regarding this specific candidate.

If the board member has something he/she wants to know more about the candidate, then he/she states what it is and the consultant makes a notation. If the candidate becomes a finalist, the consultant will formulate a question(s) regarding what the board member wants to know and will send it along as one of the questions to be asked at the site visit. As long as five board members have something they want to further discuss regarding the candidate, the candidate remains on the active final list. The consultant then turns to the audience and asks if anyone has anything else he/she wants to further know about the candidate.

If a board member does not have any further questions but wants to have the candidate remain on the list of finalists, the answer to the consultant when asked, "Do you have anything else you would like to know about this candidate?" is "I think this candidate deserves a site visit."

Upon conclusion of this session, the consultant will note if the list of original candidates interviewed has been narrowed to two or three. The consultant will then recommend that the board, by motion and vote, name the candidates as finalists and that the finalists should receive a site visit. The board then votes on the dates and times of the site visits.

If it appears to be difficult to narrow the list to two or three finalists, the board should recess again and further discuss the candidates with persons in the audience and fellow board members on an informal basis. The board will then return to session, and by motion and vote, determine the final list of candidates.

The board president then announces the names of the site visit team, which includes all of the board members available to go on the site visits, along with students, community members, and employees. Students selected are generally two juniors or seniors from the high school who have parental permission to attend the site visit. Community members who have indicated an interest to serve on the site visit team are selected by the board president. Employees are those representing each employee group in the district. If there are more than two persons from any particular employee group who indicated an interest in attending the site visit, then the employee group decides who will represent their particular group. One must keep in mind that anyone attending the site visit must have attended all interviews. The district pays for all substitutes needed for employees attending the site visits, along with other costs including transportation, housing if necessary, and food.

The consultant then gives a workshop on the procedures/guidelines for the site visit. All persons serving on the site visit team shall attend the workshop.

It must be made very clear that the site visit team members, other than board members, are an ad hoc group serving as additional eyes, ears, and feet, with the purpose of gathering additional information for the board. This group may not make any recommendations and certainly is not considered as having any part of the decision in hiring the next superintendent, which is the sole responsibility of the board.

Chapter Ten

SITE VISIT TO CANDIDATE'S WORKPLACE

The consultant will contact all candidates who were interviewed and inform each candidate of the board decision on the final candidates. As was done before, the candidates will receive a personal call from the consultant to update their individual status as a candidate, prior to any press releases.

SITE VISIT TEAM ROLE AND PROCEDURES (Ref. #33)

All persons involved in the site visits are given the following guidelines/reasons for the site visit:

1. Validate what the candidate has in his or her file and what he/she said at the interview.
2. Follow up on any further questions/concerns the board members and other team members may have.
3. Determine the candidate's relationships with employees, students, community, board, etc.
4. Leave no stone unturned. Some of the members of the visit team will follow the schedule put together by the candidate and others will talk with persons in the lunchroom, on the playground, in the halls, on the street, in stores, etc. It is the responsibility of the candidate to provide identification tags and/or passes for the site visit team members. The one thing that team members *are not* allowed to do is to interrupt the teacher(s) in the classroom.

CANDIDATE'S ROLE

The candidates who have been determined to receive a site visit will receive written guidelines from the consultant regarding the site visit. (Ref. #34)

SITE VISIT TEAM REPORT

At a scheduled board meeting, as indicated on the original calendar, the board will hear a report regarding each site visit from the site visit team. (Ref. #35)

The report should be given orally, usually by community members who attended the site visit. The report may follow the outline of the profile, may indicate the persons they talked to on the site visit, etc., and must be given in a positive nature. Any negative comments received are to be presented in a positive way. No written report should be distributed regarding the site visit as the report may be used by someone in a negative manner.

The ad hoc site visit committee *may not* make a recommendation to the board as to which candidate the board should consider hiring. However, after the reports are given, any individual who served on the site visit team may stand up and give his/her own individual recommendation. Board members do not comment on the site visit at this time.

Chapter Eleven

APPOINTMENT OF SUPERINTENDENT

After the report(s), the board should recess for a short time and talk with fellow board members and persons in the audience to obtain individual viewpoints regarding the best candidate to fill the position.

Upon returning to session, board members may give their individual viewpoints on the site visit and discuss each candidate. When the discussion has concluded, a motion should be made to offer a certain candidate the position. (Ref. #36 A)

The board president then calls the candidate, hopefully on a speakerphone, (so the audience and all board members can hear the candidate) and offers the position (all finalists will know that a phone call is going to be made). The candidate accepts the offer and then another motion is made to employ the candidate (Ref. #36B). The entire procedure should be done in this manner, as it would be very unfortunate if a board made a motion to hire a certain candidate and then not inform the candidate until the next day as the selected candidate may have accepted another position that same evening!

All other finalists who received a site visit will immediately be called and told of the board decision. Once again, the candidate will hear of the board decision from the board president directly instead of reading it in the newspaper or hearing it on the late news. Letters should be sent to all candidates who were not chosen but received an interview (Ref. #37) and all candidates who received an interview and site visit (Ref. #38).

The board president then appoints a negotiating committee to work with the new superintendent on the contract. The contract should be agreed upon and signed within one week. The candidate should not resign from his/her current position until the new contract has been signed. The board should desire to sign it quickly so that all persons will know that the position has been successfully filled. A letter should be sent to all employees as well as a press release announcing the appointment. (Ref. #39)

The current superintendent should be responsible for the transition with the new superintendent. The board should appoint a committee to plan a welcome ceremony for the new superintendent after paying tribute to the outgoing superintendent.

Chapter Twelve

GUIDELINES FOR THE "WHAT IF . . ."

1. ALL FINAL CANDIDATES WITHDRAW

This situation would be extremely unfortunate as there would be an obvious reason for this type of activity. The consultant would play an important role in assisting the board in determining the reasons for such action.

Recommendation:

A. Terminate the entire process and reevaluate the reasons why candidates withdrew.
B. Appoint an interim who will be able to assist the district in eliminating negative aspects
C. Start the process over when the district appears to have a positive perception

2. THE BOARD CANNOT AGREE TO APPOINT A CANDIDATE

No candidate should accept a position on a severe split vote of the board. With a seven-member board, the candidate may accept the position on a 6-1 vote, unlikely to accept it on a 5-2 vote, and should not accept a position on a 4-3 vote. Any candidate who accepts a position on a 4-3 vote had better plan on getting an outstanding contract and be able to retire in the near future. The superintendent position is one of uncertainty and having to cope with a split board from the beginning is difficult, at best.

However, if the board favors two top candidates and can't decide between the two, then they should invite the two top candidates back to the district for a second interview.

Recommendation:

A. Invite the top candidates back for a second interview
B. Start the process over

3. THE SELECTED CANDIDATE TURNS DOWN THE OFFER

If any candidate turns down an offer at the last minute or after he/she has officially accepted the position, then he/she has some personal and professional concerns which he/she must resolve, especially after he/she has indicated that he/she would accept the position if so offered.

The board should *not* return to the candidate list to offer the position to the second choice candidate as that is exactly what he/she would be—second choice. No superintendent should ever be reminded that he/she was the second choice.

Recommendation:

A. Hire an interim
B. Start the process over

4. THE BOARD DETERMINES THAT NO CANDIDATE IS ACCEPTABLE

If the board determines that none of the candidates interviewed will meet the needs of the district, the board has only one choice—to start the process over or hire an interim and wait six months before reposting the position.

Recommendation:

A. Start the process over
B. Hire an interim and wait six months before posting

5. THE SITE VISIT TEAM BECOMES INVOLVED IN THE DECISION-MAKING PROCESS

The consultant and the board need to remind the site visit team members that they were an ad hoc committee of the board with a specific duty to seek out information on candidates and report information back to the board. The team has *no* power to make any decision and cannot make any recommendations to the board regarding any one candidate. Only the board has the right and responsibility to make the decision to hire a specific person as the superintendent.

Recommendation:

A. Remind the team of its role
B. Make a responsible board decision

Conclusions

The selection of a new superintendent is an awesome responsibility for the board of education. The board must seek the best fit for the district, not only for the present, but for the future needs of the district. The consultant also has a great responsibility in seeking the best fit candidates for the district by determining the candidate's interest, commitment, and desire to make a difference in the community's educational system. The candidate must be able to fit the district, not try to make the district fit him or her.

Beyond The Search

Once the search is completed, the consultant may offer a board/superintendent workshop on board/superintendent roles and responsibilities to ensure that the relationship is off to a great start. (Reference #D-guarantee).

Reference (A)

COMPANY NAME

Contract for Superintendent Search

It is hereby agreed between the Board of Education of the Home Town Community Schools (hereinafter referred to as the Board) and *Name* of *Consultant, Company name* (hereinafter referred to as the Consultant) that the latter will assist the Board of Education in the selection of a Superintendent of Schools as follows:

1. The Consultant will conduct the following three seminars with the Board:

   I. At the beginning of the search to agree on all substantial details relating to the conduct of the search;
   II. At the conclusion of the input meetings for the purpose to develop a final statement of criteria for the selection for the superintendent; and
   III. At the conclusion of the consultant's screening of candidates to review the qualifications of the candidates and to assist the Board in the setting up of interviews, interview schedules, and other matters pertaining to the Board's selection process.

2. The Consultant will prepare advertisements, public announcements, and will provide a printed brochure for distribution which will detail the position available.
3. The Consultant will receive all applications, will maintain files of all applicants, will acknowledge all applications received, and will notify candidates who are not selected for the interviews.
4. The Consultant will hold input sessions with the employees of the school district, selected students, community members, and other school-related and community groups for the purpose of obtaining their recommendations for the criteria to be used in the selection of the superintendent.
5. The Consultant will prepare for the Board a summary of the recommendations received from the input session.
6. On the basis of the Board's determination of the criteria to be utilized, the Consultant will prepare the statement of the criteria and disseminate the statement to all potential candidates for the position.
7. The Consultant will screen the credentials of all applicants, will obtain additional information about applicants as appears desirable, and will classify all applicants into two groups:

   I. Those applicants who meet the qualifications established by the Board and are considered worthy of consideration;

   II. Those applicants who do not meet the qualifications established by the Board.

8. Credentials of all candidates will be reviewed with the Board in a seminar to be held with the Board as indicated in Items 1-2 above.

9. The Consultant will assist the Board in the establishment of the interview guidelines and the scheduling of interviews. The Consultant will be present at the interviews to assist the Board as called upon.

10. __(Company name)__ will conduct their responsibilities in accordance with professional standards and acceptable principles of personnel management and will observe all state laws and Equal Opportunity rules and regulations.

11. This contract shall be completed either upon the employment of the Superintendent by the Board from the list of qualified candidates, or the Board's rejection of all candidates. The Consultant will, at the Board's request, conduct a further posting and screening of candidates. The cost of further postings and screenings shall be agreed upon prior to the start of such activities.

12. Payment for the above services shall be $_____ which includes all of the Consultant's expenses.

Payments by the Board shall be made to __(Company name)__ as follows:

(4 partial payments on specific dates)

Signed in __City__, __State__, this _____ day of _____, 20__.

Approved for the Home Town Community Schools by the Board of Education at a special meeting on the _____ day of _____, 20__.

COMPANY NAME

By: _____ Title: _____

HOME TOWN COMMUNITY SCHOOLS

By: _____ Title: _____

By: _____ Title: _____

Reference (B)

LETTER HEAD STATIONERY

Board of Education
Home Town Community Schools
Address
City, State

Dear Board Members,

Please accept this letter as an indication of our interest in providing independent consulting services for the Home Town Community Schools Superintendent search.

Our services include obtaining input from designated groups, developing a profile to meet the needs of the district, posting the position, receiving and acknowledging applications, communicating with the candidates to verify the contents of their individual application packets, checking references, providing the board with a workshop on the interview process and proposed interview questions, attending the interviews, and setting up site visits. We also assist the board with negotiations regarding the new superintendent's contract, if the board so desires. We provide a one-year guarantee that the new superintendent and board will have a good start on a successful board/superintendent working relationship. The key to our process is to assist the board in finding the best match for the district. We do not have a designated list of candidates which we try to place in administrative positions as every district is unique and has specific needs to be fulfilled. We provide a true search service; we are not a placement service.

A typical timeline is ten weeks (8 weeks minimum) from the start of the search to the signing of the contract with the new superintendent. Our total fee for the complete search is $_____ with no added costs.

Our process also provides the board some flexibility to add or modify search services as needed.

Recent searches which we have completed are *given in a list along with names of references.*

We will be pleased to discuss the enclosed proposal with you.

We are looking forward to hearing from you in the near future.

Sincerely,

(Consultant's name)

Reference (C)

LETTERHEAD STATIONERY

Board of Education
Home Town Community Schools
Address
City, State

Dear Board Members:

The following proposal is presented as an indication of our interest in providing independent consulting services for the Home Town Community Schools Superintendent Search.

A general outline of consulting services, which we would provide, is as follows:

1. A meeting with the Board of Education to determine:

   a. Scope of the search
      (local, state, regional, national)
   b. Timelines for the search (calendar)
   c. Guidelines for posting position

2. Hold input meetings with designated groups.
3. After obtaining input, meet with the Board of Education to establish a profile for the position.
4. Production of a brochure/web site information
5. Post position and network with others to secure applications.
6. Receive and acknowledge applications.
7. Screen all applications to determine that established criteria are met.
8. Follow up on candidate references.
9. Screen all applications and categorize them.
10. Meet with/contact all top candidates on an individual basis to validate information in the files and obtain any additional information.
11. Meet with the Board to review *all* applications and give recommendations to the board.
12. Board determines candidates to interview.
13. Schedule candidates for interview.

14. Conduct a workshop for the Board regarding the interview procedures.
15. Establish list of questions directly related to the profile for the Board of Education to use as a guideline.
16. Provide a rating form to be used by each board member at the completion of each interview.
17. Board determines final candidates.
18. Schedule Board Committee visits to place of candidate's employment. Assist the board visitation team with questions to ask and identify specific persons to visit.
19. Meet with the Board to hear report of the site visit team. Board determines if a specific candidate is to be offered a contract.
20. If a decision is not made during the previous step, then schedule the specifically designated final candidate(s) for a second interview with the Board and other groups if desired.

The above service will be provided in a timely and professional manner for the fee of $_____ which covers *all* of the consultant's expenses.

Please feel free to contact us at _____ (cellular) or _____ (office) for further information and/or to further discuss our consulting services, which we believe would meet your needs.

Sincerely,

Name of Consultant

Reference (D)

SAMPLE

GUARANTEE REGARDING PLACEMENT

1. Once the details of the procedures for the search are finalized between __(company name)__ and the board, __(company name)__ will implement the search and handle all the responsibilities as outlined until a candidate is selected by the Board of Education.

2. __(Company name)__ will conduct an introductory meeting between the new superintendent and the board if deemed appropriate by the Board of Education. This meeting would facilitate a review of district concerns and lay out suggested responsibilities of the parties to ensure a smooth and effective administrative transition.

3. Should serious problems develop between the new superintendent and the Board of Education during the first year of appointment, we will conduct a meeting between the parties in an effort to help resolve the problems. The meeting would be held only if the Board of Education desired such an approach.

4. Should the new superintendent and Board of Education determine to sever their relationship within one year of the appointment, __(company name)__ will reestablish the original search agreement between __(company name)__ and the Board of Education and seek a replacement candidate for expenses-only cost to the school district.

Reference # 1

QUESTIONS FOR SEARCH FIRMS:

1. How many searches have you *personally* completed?
2. How many searches is your firm involved in at the present time?
3. How many persons work in your firm?
4. How many searches has your firm done in which a board did not find a candidate on the first round of interviews?
5. What is the "staying power" of the candidates in the districts you have done the search?
6. What kind of guarantee do you provide the board?
7. How many women and minorities have been hired in searches you have conducted?
8. How involved does the community and employees get in your process?
9. What makes your service better than everyone else?
10. Why should we hire you?
11. What is the most important part of the process which you provide?
12. Do you personally interview (face-to-face) all top candidates?
13. What kind of follow up do you do after the candidate is appointed?
14. How much communication with the employees, students, and community do you provide?
15. How do you deal with inside candidates?
16. Why should a board hire a search firm?

Reference # 2

HOME TOWN COMMUNITY SCHOOLS
BOARD OF EDUCATION
SUPERINTENDENT SEARCH
CALENDAR

Mar 8	Consultants meet with Board of Education to set search guidelines
Mar 9	Post position
Mar 7-9	Meet with designated groups for input
Mar 14	Meet with the Board of Education to approve criteria for profile
Mar 15	Brochure completed
April 12	All applications are to be received by the consultants no later than 4:00 p.m. (EST) on April 12, 20__
Apr 14-18	All applications are screened by consultants and individual board members
Apr 18	Board meets in closed session to review all candidate credentials with consultants (5:30 p.m.). (All candidate credential files will be available to board members by April 14, 20__.) Board determines candidates to be interviewed.
Apr 22-23	Initial interviews
Apr 26-28	Board/committee visitation to candidate's work place
May 2	Board meets to hear visitation team reports
May 2*	Board appoints new superintendent
July 1, 20__	New superintendent assumes position.

*If more time is needed, appointment may be rescheduled.

Reference # 3

SALARY STATISTICS INFORMATION . . .

Attached is the current information regarding superintendent salaries for the school year 20__-20__.

The districts listed are those which are members of the same athletic league and other districts to which I understand you often compare or relate to your district.

My suggestion for the determination of a base salary is $_____ with no deferred compensation (TSA). The base of $_____ will allow you some room for adding additional dollars or a TSA if necessary. It is a fair salary and will attract well-qualified candidates. Please keep in mind that the salaries provided are for the 20__-20__ (current) school year and the salary you will be determining is for the 20__-20__ (next) school year.

I am also recommending a three-year contract.

Please feel free to call if you have need for any further information or have any questions.

(Consultant's name)

HOME TOWN COMMUNITY SCHOOLS
SUPERINTENDENT SEARCH
SALARY STUDY INFORMATION
FEBRUARY 2, 20__

School	Enroll	Salary	TSA	Total
"B"	7200	$116,912	$6,000	$122,912
"C"	2876	$119,067	$13,000	$132,067
"D"	3481	$110,000	$5,500	$115,500
"F"	3151	$104,059	$4,000	$108,059
"H"	5330	$114,154	$5,708	$119,862
"H"	8579	$140,000	$5,000	$145,000
"S"	5415	$112,192	$7,500	$119,692
Home Town	4928	$133,908	$-0-	$133,908

AVERAGES: All Districts
    $118,787 without TSA
    $124,625 with TSA

TSA=amount of tax sheltered annuity or deferred compensation paid by the board

(SCHOOL LETTERHEAD)

Announcement of Opening

POSITION:	Superintendent of Schools
LOCATION:	Home Town Community Schools Home Town, USA
DESCRIPTION:	Located along the shores of the Big Pine River on the extreme southern fringe of the Big Pine Metropolitan Suburban Area. K-12 NCA accredited K-12 enrollment 4782
EDUCATIONAL REQUIREMENT:	Must meet North Central Requirements
DATE TO BEGIN DUTIES:	July 1, 20__
CONTRACT:	$120,000 base salary Three-year contract Customary fringe package
CLOSING DATE FOR COMPLETED APPLICATION.	All applications must be received by the consultant no later than 4:00 p.m. (EST) on April 12, 20__
SEND LETTER OF INTEREST, RESUME, AND CREDENTIALS TO:	(Consultant's name) (address) (phone) (fax) (e-mail)

Reference # 5

SUGGESTED ADVERTISING

National Organizations

- American Association of School Administrators (AASA)
  Web Site (Most responses)

- National School Board Association (NSBA)

- Various State Associations
  Publications and web sites

Publications

- Education Week

- Local Newspapers

Various Web Sites

- Organizations listed above

- District Web Site

Reference # 6

GROUPS TO BE SCHEDULED FOR INPUT SESSIONS

Employee groups
Elementary teaching staff
Middle/Jr. High School teaching staff
High School teaching staff
Preschool, Adult Education and Community Education teaching staff
Secretaries
Para Pros (Aides)
Maintenance/Custodial
Bus drivers
Food service
Directors
Principals
Central office personnel—support
Central office personnel—administrators

School Groups
Students (usually student council officers)
Booster and band clubs
PTA/PTO/Parent volunteers
School Improvement teams

Community groups
Service clubs (Rotary, Lions, Chamber of Commerce, etc.)
Senior citizens

NOTE: All groups should be given at least one-half hour for the session, and enough time should be allowed between sessions for the consultant to travel and set up.

The community meetings (one in the morning, one in the afternoon and one in the evening) should be set for one hour with the beginning and ending times stated.

Supervisors/Administrators should not attend meetings other than their own and board members should not attend any meetings. (Board's input is scheduled for another time.)

All community groups not having a special session with the consultants should be sent a copy of the citizen's letter from the board president inviting them to a general session for community input.

Reference # 7

HOME TOWN COMMUNITY SCHOOLS
SUPERINTENDENT SEARCH
INPUT GROUP SCHEDULE

TUESDAY, MARCH 7, 20__

7:15-7:45	a.m.	HIGH SCHOOL TEACHERS
8:15-8:45	a.m.	"B" ELEMENTARY
9:15-9:45	a.m.	TRANSPORTATION
1:15-1:45	p.m.	FOOD SERVICE
2:45-3:15	p.m.	MIDDLE SCHOOL TEACHERS
4:00-4:15	p.m.	"T" ELEMENTARY TEACHERS
7:00-8:00	p.m.	BOARD OF EDUCATION
8:00-9:00	p.m.	COMMUNITY

WEDNESDAY, MARCH 8, 20__

8:00-8:30	a.m.	"G" INTERMEDIATE
9:00-9:30	a.m.	CENTRAL OFFICE SUPPORT STAFF
12:00-12:30	p.m.	"R" ELEMENTARY
1:00-1:30	p.m.	ADMINISTRATORS/DIRECTORS
4:00-5:00	p.m.	COMMUNITY MEETING

THURSDAY, MARCH 9, 20_

| 11:15-11:45 | a.m. | HIGH SCHOOL STUDENT SENATE |
| 12:00 | noon | ROTARY |

TO BE PRINTED ON SCHOOL LETTERHEAD

_____, 20__

Dear Home Town Community Schools Employee:

As you are aware, the Home Town Community Schools District is in the process of selecting a new superintendent. As a part of the plan to select our next superintendent, your school board has solicited the professional expertise of _(consultant and company name)_ to assist with this critical decision-making process. An important element in the overall plan is to receive valuable input from school employees. Therefore, we are seeking ideas as to the characteristics you would like our new superintendent to possess.

Although there may be a wide range of opinions regarding needed superintendent characteristics, _(consultant and company name)_ will submit your list of potential attributes to the Board of Education for assistance in finalizing the needed characteristics in our next superintendent. She plans to be in the school district on _(dates)_ to meet with various employee groups. Please check the enclosed schedule for the times she will be available to receive your ideas. In the event you cannot attend the meeting time scheduled for your particular group, please feel free to attend a different session to give your valuable input.

If you would prefer, you may give your comments in writing. Any written suggestions/comments should be sent to: _(consultant and company name)_ c/o Superintendent's Office, Home Town Community Schools. Written response needs to be received no later than noon on March 2, 20__.

On behalf of our entire Board of Education, thank you for your interest and contribution to the education of Home Town Community Schools Students.

Sincerely,

(President's name and signature)

Reference # 9

TO BE PRINTED ON SCHOOL LETTERHEAD

_____, 20__

Dear Citizens:

As you are aware, the Home Town Community Schools District is in the process of selecting a new superintendent. As a part of the plan to select our next superintendent, your school board has solicited the professional expertise of __(consultant and company name)__ to assist with this critical decision-making process. An important element in the overall plan is to receive valuable input from community members. Therefore, we are seeking ideas as to the characteristics you would like our new superintendent to possess.

Although there may be a wide range of opinions regarding needed superintendent characteristics, _(consultant and company name)_ will submit your list of potential attributes to the Board of Education for assistance in finalizing the needed characteristics in our next superintendent. She will meet with community citizens at _____, February _____, 20__, and March _____ 20__, in the _____.

If you would prefer, you may give your comments in writing. Any written suggestions/comments should be sent to: __(consultant and company name)__ c/o Superintendent's Office, Home Town Community Schools. Written response needs to be received no later than noon, March 2, 20__.

On behalf of our entire Board of Education, thank you for your interest and contribution to the education of Home Town Community Schools Students.

Sincerely,

(President's name and signature)

HOME TOWN COMMUNITY SCHOOLS
SUPERINTENDENT PROFILE
PROFILE CHARACTERISTICS—INPUT SESSIONS

THE FOLLOWING IS A LISTING OF COMMENTS MADE DURING THE INPUT SESSIONS:

- good leader
- honest, up front
- tells it like it is
- a Joe clone (current superintendent)
- good communicator
- excellent public relations person
- positive person
- will seek programs for gifted and talented students
- fiscally responsible
- conservative with the dollars
- experienced in and knowledgeable of the legislative process
- supports all special needs programs
- evaluates the need for drug education and discipline at the high school
- always keeps kids first
- likes kids
- fiscally responsible
- approachable/available
- communicates well with all persons
- works well with local governmental agencies and the community as a whole
- will listen and act upon requests in a timely manner and then follow through
- a strong person
- compassionate
- supports a discipline policy which is implemented fairly and consistently throughout the system
- ensures that teachers are attentive to individual student needs—especially at the high school
- holds all employees accountable
- highly visible and involved in all school facilities—knows what is going on

- ensures that special-needs students receive the necessary service and that parents know what is available for students and parents
- a good listener—hears what is said
- involved in special education—knows what is going on
- approachable/available
- visible and involved in the community
- ensures that discipline policies are implemented fairly and consistently throughout the district
- brings back the high school parent group and address their concerns regarding such topics as substance abuse
- honest, up front
- knows what is going on throughout the district
- able to acknowledge and deal with difficult issues
- keeps kids first
- knows kids by first names
- truly cares about kids
- is a Joe clone
- will get rid of junk food throughout the district
- a positive person
- highly visible and involved in the community
- positive person
- communicates well and often with parents
- has a high level of integrity
- honest, tells it like it is
- energetic
- willing to spend the necessary time on the job
- fiscally responsible
- conservative
- experienced in and knowledgeable of the legislative process
- Joe clone
- keeps kids first—always!
- will build a team with local governmental agencies
- is collaborative with local governmental agencies—i.e., grants, programs, etc.
- actively engaged with young people
- ability to build a strong team with the local agencies—assists and looks out for each other
- a strong community connector for kids
- work cooperatively with local, state, and federal governmental agencies
- ability to build a strong network
- a positive person

- likes kids
- keeps kids first, always
- sense of humor
- compassionate but strong
- respects and values teachers and all other employees
- fiscally responsible
- creative at funding programs
- works with the public libraries, cooperative ventures
- recognizes that teachers are a highly intelligent group balanced with logic and a heart
- listens to teachers
- trusts teachers to know what is best for kids
- realizes that teachers are an incredible group of people, a team of people who will work with the superintendent
- relies upon teachers to help problem-solve instead of looking at teachers as a problem
- will trust teachers and teachers can trust him/her
- has relevant teaching experience
- embraces the team approach—not top-down management
- empowers site-based decision making
- willing to bargain collaboratively
- needs to understand the roles of the seven elected school board members and administrators
- understands the role of extracurricular activities as a part of the educational process—"co" curricular
- works politically for funding with the state government
- is willing to support teachers
- strong understanding of secondary changes in graduation requirements
- someone from outside the district with a fresh perspective
- extended relevant classroom experience not too far removed from current times
- good problem solver who makes use of input from different groups
- genuine and a good fit with the community
- is willing to understand that we aren't perfect and addresses the problem head-on rather than sweeping it under the carpet
- one who will actually empower administrators to act in the best interests of their staffs—deal with conflicts at the building level—site based management
- refers parents to the building principals before going to the superintendent—chain of command
- values administrators and their role in the district

- seeks, values, and listens to the recommendations of committees
- is not a micromanager
- gives credit where credit is due—doesn't take all the credit himself/herself
- is not a consummate politician—tells it like it is—doesn't sugarcoat issues
- sincere and honest
- values and respects teachers
- encourages dialogue between board members and teachers
- has experience as a successful superintendent
- knows how to work positively with teachers, administrators, and parents
- is not ego-centered
- is someone from outside of the district with no ties to the district
- is grounded in reality, not fantasy
- does not view education as a consumer transaction where the customer is always right
- views the school district as a theatrical production:
  o understands that everyone makes a contribution to the success or failure of the production
  o understands that each and every person in a school district has a role, whether it be on or off stage
  o allows everyone the autonomy to perform his or her job
  o understands that the student and the parent are as responsible for the final production as are the players on the stage
- good with kids
- likes kids
- personable
- intelligent
- well-educated
- strong person—able to make a decision
- friendly
- outgoing
- sense of humor
- likes kids
- knows kids and they know him/her
- honest, up front
- will enforce policies
- high integrity
- honest
- has good rapport with community
- available/approachable

- likes kids
- communicates well with all employees and students
- highly visible and involved in all schools
- Joe clone
- personable
- up front, honest
- supports kids
- stands strong on what is right
- listens to parents
- relates well to kids—understands their current issues
- honest, up front
- ability to handle conflict
- open-minded
- ensures that discipline policies are implemented fairly and consistently throughout the district
- conservative
- on the job when needed
- a good leader
- has a vested interest in kids
- high morals, integrity
- honest, tells it like it is
- relates well with all employees
- stands up for and supports teachers—i.e., parent concerns
- ensures that all discipline policies are implemented fairly and consistently throughout the district
- open-minded
- honest, tells it like it is
- handles conflict honestly and timely—i.e., high school student concerns
- seeks and values input in the decision making process, especially from those directly involved
- a Joe clone
- strong beliefs in discipline
- high morals, values, ethics, religion, and academics
- involved leader in the community
- open to teachers and parents
- holds students accountable for their actions
- must enforce zero tolerance of drugs, alcohol, enforce a dress code, a behavioral code, and *zero* tolerance of gun possession
- encourages parents to get involved in the discipline of their children
- professional
- compassionate

- puts the needs of the community first-helping all kids
- will live in the community
- earns and maintains the trust of the community, teachers, and administration by exemplifying strong leadership qualities
- unwavering decision making must be communicated extremely well
- visible and accessible to develop an understanding within the school environment
- able to show that the concerns and opinions of others are seriously taken into consideration and explains why things were acted upon or why they were not without creating hostility and animosity
- has a strong voice and tie into the state government i.e., school funding
- finds and utilizes the local brain power and talent within the district for the invention of ideas, solutions, and dreams that are most pertinent to the district
- will have more than two years teaching experience
- from outside of the district—a fresh approach
- personable, outgoing
- approachable/available
- involved in the legislative process
- good manager
- involved in building positive relationships with local governmental agencies
- develops a partnership with parents/teachers/students—"school family"
- able to deal with conflict in a positive and timely manner
- open-minded
- understands and knows curriculum—especially ours
- encourages others, doesn't push
- seeks, values, and appreciates input in the decision-making process from all persons, especially from those directly involved
- a collaborative leader
- knows our district
- encourages parental involvement
- good public relations skills
- visionary—with a focus
- excellent communicator
- has excellent follow through skills
- highly visible and involved in the community
- able to build a team in the community to develop resources for kids
- seeks out creative funding sources
- promotes the positive—champion the district

- able to handle difficult situations in a positive and timely manner
- honest, up front
- tells it like it is
- a good listener—hears what is said and acknowledge it
- open—minded
- not a slick politician
- stands up for what is right
- knowledgeable and experienced in the legislative process at the local, state, and national levels—i.e. grants, resources,
- collaborative
- approachable/available
- knows kids and kids know him/her
- highly visible and involved in all school facilities—attends school activities PK-12—knows what is going on
- understands our community
- wants to be here
- knowledgeable and experienced in all curriculum areas—"ours"
- HTESA—understands it and its function
- understands and supports special-needs programs
- ensures that the needs of *all* children are met
- allows each person to do his/her job—does not micromanage
- builds a strong school team
- strong leader
- able to make a decision and follow through in a timely manner
- treats all persons equally and with respect
- return calls promptly
- knows persons names
- highly visible at school activities, PK-12
- encourages all persons to reach his/her potential
- highly visible and involved in all school facilities—knows what is going on
- appreciates and values all employees
- good listener—"hears"
- child friendly
- likes kids
- ensures that all students' needs are met
- appreciates and values the Home Town Community Education Center/ Preschool—involves employees in all programs
- no empty promises
- honest, up front
- understands and supports early childhood education

- realizes that kids serviced by HTESA in Home Town are all HTCS students
- current on educational issues and research and supports those which will meet the needs of HTCS students
- willing to deal with problems—doesn't sweep them under the rug
- works collaboratively with all employees
- has a positive track record in win-win negotiations
- supports a "living" contract
- understands the role of the Board of Education and superintendent.
- from outside of the district—a fresh look at the district
- highly visible and involved in all school facilities—knows what is going on
- has a long-term vision for the district—how education is going to change in the twenty-first century
- understands and has firsthand knowledge of classroom needs and activities—i.e. involving teachers, parents, and students
- looks at all sides of the problem and makes a decision which is best for kids
- wants to be here
- makes a commitment to HTCS
- knows and gets involved in the legislative process—school funding
- from outside of the district—gives a fresh look
- has a positive track record in collaborative bargaining
- highly visible and involved in all school facilities—PK-12, knows what is going on
- builds and fosters a strong team concept throughout the district—"school family"
- seeks, values, and appreciates input in the decision making process, especially from those directly involved and then follow through in a timely manner
- treats all persons with dignity and respect even in conflict
- involved in the legislative process at the state level—school funding
- fiscally responsible—spends dollars wisely only on needed materials, seeks input on needs
- experienced and knowledgeable in PK-12 curriculum, knows what is going on, seeks input/support with money, materials, staff
- has teachers give input on needed professional development
- reinstitute the K-12 curriculum council
- appreciates and values all persons' talents and expertise, utilize, and say thanks
- support site-based decision making
- an excellent problem solver

- takes responsibility for decisions
- admits to making a mistake
- available/approachable
- experienced/knowledgeable of all special needs programs—special education, mainstream, gifted and talented, etc.—recognizes that each area has different needs, no program fits all kids
- each student should be encouraged to reach his/her potential
- supports fair and consistent discipline across the system
- open communication with parents and the community—concise and timely
- ensure that parents know what programs outside of school, such as at the HTRSA, are available for HTCS students, i.e., alternative programs
- fiscally responsible and seeks and values ideas and opinions regarding priorities
- ensure that the core curriculum is defined, justified, and clearly communicated to parents and community
- highly visible and involved in all schools, activities, and the community as a whole
- has a presence in the community
- not a rubber stamp to the teacher union
- visionary—with a focus
- likes kids
- politically involved with state legislature—lets them know about HTCS needs
- fiscally responsible, understands the budget
- a team builder and participant
- has a positive track record of "customer service"
- a Joe clone
- does not have his/her own agenda
- open, honest, trustworthy
- tells it like it is
- integrity
- dynamic, enthusiastic
- a good leader
- encourages others
- gives praise where it is due—in an honest way
- gives positive reinforcement
- treats all employees fairly and equally
- seeks alternative funding, additional revenue—creative
- ability to build a critical network in community
- open to all ideas

- seeks, values, and appreciates input in the decision making process, especially from those directly involved
- sincere personality
- honest, up front
- tells it like it is
- supports *all* employees—i.e. "school family"
- supports a collaborative environment
- support student needs services
- is current on educational issues and research
- highly visible in all school facilities, knows what is going on
- ensures that all buildings are treated equally and fairly—i.e., budget, materials, staff, etc
- ensures that all administrators serve as a team
- proven track record of ethical conduct
- realizes that different areas of our community have different needs—i.e., social, economic, etc
- fosters respect, encouragement to all persons
- holds all persons accountable, follows through
- strong supporter of all arts including athletics, physical education, considers a new stadium, etc.
- ensure that drugs are kept out of our school—-takes action, ensures implementation of discipline policies
- excellent communicator with all persons
- open, honest, tells it like it is
- communicates the "schools" to the public
- experience in a similar district—i.e., size, etc.
- ability to be a good time manager, gets things done
- will communicate with students on a regular basis
- excellent public relations person
- able to make decisions and follows through
- willing and able to delegate
- highly visible and involved in all school activities at all levels
- is a good fit for our district
- wants to be here
- not ego-centered
- open to new ideas
- does not bend to pressure groups/individuals
- sense of humor
- highly visible in all school facilities, knows what is going on
- keeps kids first—always
- takes pride in his/her position
- involved in community organizations, service groups, etc

- energetic, healthy, able to focus
- down-to-earth, common
- doesn't plan to change things for change's sake, takes time for evaluation, assessment, then implements those changes which benefit kids
- will not bend to pressure groups/individuals
- willing to empower administrators
- treats all persons equally and fairly
- encourages and promotes site-based decision making and follow through
- is *not* a micromanager
- is not ego-centered
- values the work of committees
- sincere, frank, honest
- values and respects teachers
- has previous experience as a superintendent
- works well with teachers
- fiscally responsible—deals with reality
- respects and values each person's talents, expertise, utilizes, and says thanks
- believes that student activities are "co" curricular, not "extra" curricular
- keeps a professional relationship with the board—employer, employee
- works with all community groups, not just his/her favorites
- knowledgeable of all new graduation requirements
- will support and promote athletics-facilities, materials, staff, etc
- able to make a decision and follow through
- supports competition-i.e., athletics
- instills pride in HTCS
- promotes internal pride-employees/students
- carefully weighs short-term gain vs. long-term consequences
- upholds and maintains healthy principles set forth by principals/administrators and school board
- seeks, values, and appreciates each person's ideas and opinions in the decision making process, especially from those directly involved
- knowledgeable and experienced with special needs programs
- current on educational research and issues
- will not bend to pressure groups/individuals
- will deal with problems, conflict at the high school
- will not sweep problems, concerns under the rug
- makes a commitment to HTCS—will stay a while
- understands the uniqueness of our district

- highly visible and involved in the community
- people person
- open-minded
- doesn't come with his/her own agenda
- good listener—"hears"
- available/approachable
- collaborative leader
- inclusive decision maker
- fiscally responsible
- a hockey fan
- involved in the legislative process, especially in school finance
- sense of humor
- common, down-to-earth
- current on educational issues and research and supports those that will make a difference for HTCS
- vision regarding student success
- visionary—with a focus
- doesn't make change for change's sake
- servant leader
- encourages each person to reach his/her potential
- forward thinking
- models collaborative leadership
- understanding of a data-driven culture
- builds capacity for leadership in buildings
- believes in and supports site-based management
- fosters new leadership from within
- empowers employees
- sees the whole picture
- relates well to support staff
- committed to establishing community relationships and partnerships
- keeps kids first—always
- highly visible and involved in all school facilities and the community
- walks on water especially if it is frozen
- values all programs equally—i.e., arts and athletics
- someone who will say a while
- will live here
- experienced in and understanding of the learning community
- creative problem solver
- flexible
- ensures a safe environment for all students
- understands and embraces the value of technology
- recognizes the need for intervention when necessary

- a colleague of the administrative team
- team builder and participant
- fosters open dialogue
- seeks, values, and appreciates input in the decision making process, especially from those directly involved
- not self-centered
- ensures that the chain of command is followed
- strong leader in curriculum and instruction
- has K-12 experience
- values elementary
- will move to the community
- has a connrioution with fids
- team builder and participant
- does direct deposit of his/her check
- a Joe clone
- personable
- decisive
- highly visible and involved in the community
- motivator
- fair, honest
- high integrity
- not in midlife crisis
- approachable/available
- returns phone calls promptly
- responsive
- commitment to HTCS—will stay a while
- kind, considerate
- seeks and values input in the decision making process, especially from those directly involved
- appreciates honesty—agree to disagree, agreeably
- sense of humor
- kids first, always
- communicates with the transportation department
- stay a while
- seek and value input in the decision making process, especially from those directly involved
- highly visible and involved in all school facilities, knows what is going on
- sense of humor
- outgoing
- compassionate
- understanding

- treats all persons fairly and equally
- thinks out of the box—creative
- honest, up front, tells it like it is
- supports *all* employees
- has five to ten years experience in the classroom
- not a micromanager
- lets each person do his/her job
- open-door policy
- appreciates the "tenor" of the central office staff—"school family"
- highly visible and involved in all school facilities and the community as a whole
- builds and fosters relationships with families
- lives here
- master of curriculum and instruction
- knowledgeable of all federal and state programs and requirements
- works well with the Board of Education
- works collaboratively with the HTESA and other governmental and community agencies
- involved in the legislative process at the state level
- genuine, be himself/herself
- professional at all times
- ability to deal with conflict in a positive manner
- kid focused—always
- makes decisions in the kid's best interest
- communicates well with parents
- returns calls promptly
- not a micromanager
- stay awhile
- classroom experience in last ten years
- elementary experience
- gets to know all employees
- highly visible and involved in all school facilities, knows what is going on
- support small (20-22) class sizes in elementary
- supports materials, time and money for *all* student needs
- open, honest
- communicates well with all employees
- organized
- starts something and follows through
- seeks and values input in the decision making process, especially from those directly involved
- makes a decision and follows through

- supports *all* employees—not just parents
- views employees as stakeholders
- listens to all sides of an issue before making decisions
- from outside of the district
- track record in positive labor relations, including negotiations
- deals in reality—doesn't overwhelm
- doesn't push but will encourage
- will take us from good to great
- will "grow our own" leaders
- mentors and encourages new leaders
- good strategic planner
- fiscally responsible
- excellent people skills
- open, honest
- will deal with conflicts and concerns at the high school
- assesses employee strengths and talents and hold all persons accountable
- visionary—with a focus
- seek Blue Ribbon status and NCA for all schools
- stands up for his/her convictions, beliefs
- realizes the difference in students at the middle level and supports with money, materials, staff to meet all student needs
- understands and supports special needs programs
- support all employees, not just the parents
- from outside the district—fresh look
- take us from where we are and go on to great heights
- sincere, honest
- has recent classroom experience
- involved in the legislative process
- stay a while
- supports the "school family" concept
- treats all employees equally and fairly
- treats all levels (K-12) equally and fairly—core curriculum and support before "fun" classes
- understands and supports technology and its role in schools for today and tomorrow—updated
- treats all persons professionally
- seeks, values, and appreciates input in the decision-making process, especially from those persons directly involved
- approachable/available
- highly visible in all school facilities—knows what is going on
- follows chain of command and ensures that others do the same

- supports athletics
- treats elective programs as core programs
- visionary—with a focus
- doesn't make change for change's sake
- from outside of the district
- sincere
- honest, up front
- listens—"hears"
- team builder and participant
- works well with the Board of Education
- highly visible and involved at all school activities at all levels K-12
- highly visible in classrooms—knows what is going on
- understands elementary education
- has recent classroom experience
- kids first, always
- visionary—with a focus
- creative
- involved in the legislative process—at the local and state levels
- ability to delegate and hold all persons accountable
- understands and supports curriculum
- fiscally responsible
- honest, up front, tells it like it is with all persons
- supportive of all employees
- works effectively with all persons
- seeks, values, and appreciates input in the decision making process, especially from those directly involved
- a person who has teaching experience within a reasonable amount of time from the present
- a fresh perspective to how things can be managed effectively
- someone who is willing to work in every building with the staff to support our district goals
- willing to work with and support the teachers in our quest for educational excellence
- a team player—realizes that teachers are with the students every day and that teachers have the vital role in students' education
- will work with teachers and not against them in serving the needs of students
- empowers the buildings to use site-based decision making and backs up the people who do so
- is interested in becoming an intricate part in the team of people striving for excellence in Home Town and does not put himself/herself on a pedestal above the others working with him/her

- wants to collaborate with all of the parties affected in decision making
- is able to work politically to change the inadequacies in education programs
- understands curriculum issues and works toward solutions
- has a genuine emotion for the students and people of Home Town
- will always strive to meet the needs of this district and the people who live in it
- relevant teaching experience
- embraces the team approach
- empowers site-based decision making
- willing to bargain collaboratively
- has a good understanding about the roles of the elected school board members and administrators
- understands the role of extracurricular programs as part of the educational process
- works politically for funding with the state government
- willing to support the teachers
- strong understanding of secondary changes in graduation requirements
- from outside of the district with a fresh perspective
- good problem solver
- seeks input from different groups
- genuine
- a good fit with the community
- willing to understand that Home Town isn't perfect and addresses the problem head-on rather than sweeping it under the carpet
- creative thinker
- sees the big picture
- open communication—"in-house" people should know what is going on before they read it in the newspaper
- keeps kids first
- approachable, open door
- not a micromanager
- technology user
- innovative
- courteous and responsive
- high energy
- honest
- sense of humor
- ability to keep the momentum this district has achieved going forward
- recognizes the potential and possibility in all students
- realizes that special education is a service and support, not a place

- understands that Least Restrictive Environment is about accessing the general education curriculum
- teachers must have professional development to support "inclusion"
- realize that disability is the largest minority in our district
- has a "can do vs. can't do" attitude around inclusion, LRE, students with disabilities
- knows that IDELA doesn't mean separate or segregated classrooms because that is the way it has always been done—it isn't about funding
- has the heart and mind to see all students as learners
- recognizes, practices, and honors diversity
- looks at disability as possibilities instead of negative attributes
- does not bend to pressure groups/individuals
- available/approachable
- current on educational issues and research and promotes and supports those which will make a difference for HTCS students
- wants to be here, will live here, become involved in the community
- just like Joe: one mood all the time—every day is a good day
- decision making
- makes every decision as a well-thought-out decision
- no "knee jerk" reaction based on what is most expedient, popular, or self-serving
- makes decisions that are the best for the organization in the long term, not a particular employee or group
- makes decisions that are best for the kids—not a particular employee or group
- treats differing opinions with respect and takes all points of view into consideration in decision making (collaborative-team)
- consistency, honesty, integrity
- sense of humor
- down to earth
- has great communication skills
- track record of "going to bat" for public education with legislators—needs to fight for equity for under-funded districts
- committed to becoming very visible and involved in the Home Town Community—need to know the "players" and build relationships—must build goodwill with other organizations, local governments, businesses, etc.
- must "play nice" in the sandbox—no one likes a bully, it's not an effective leadership style
- accessible to parents, staff, and community members—open door

- supports technology and its integration into all aspects of the curriculum—supports replacement of obsolete equipment as a priority as prudently allowed by the budget
- hires good people and allows them to do their jobs—doesn't micromanage
- needs to have a strong curriculum background and a strong understanding of school finance
- doesn't bend to pressure groups/individuals
- current on educational issues and research

HOME TOWN COMMUNITY SCHOOLS
SUPERINTENDENT PROFILE
FREQUENCY LISTINGS

The number in parenthesis () indicates the number of times that individual statement or one similar in meaning was stated. These statements reflect the summary of input given during eighteen scheduled sessions, numerous impromptu sessions and several written communications with approximately 370 participants . . .

The superintendent leadership skills, characteristics, personal traits shall include the following:

- honest; trustworthy; integrity; ethical; high morals; tells it like it is; sincere (49)
- likes kids; keeps kids first, always (37)
- will build a "team" concept throughout the school system; supports administrators; does not micromanage; has high expectations of all persons; delegates and holds each person accountable; treats all persons equally, fairly, and with respect; promotes the concept of "school family" (36)
- a strong supporter of curriculum and instruction; seeks to meet the needs of *all* students, including those in special programs; treat all programs equally and fairly throughout the system; keeps academic achievement as a top priority (35)
- people person; kind, caring, considerate; energetic; enthusiastic; down-to-earth; common (31)
- excellent communicator with all persons; a good listener; promotes an open door policy; a good public relations person (30)
- appreciates and values all persons talents and expertise; values, respects, and supports all employees; relates well with all employees (28)
- appreciates and values the uniqueness of our community—will make a commitment, live in our community, and stay a while; wants to be here (26)
- highly visible in all school facilities; attends student activities at all levels; known by all students; knows what is going on (23)
- seeks and values input in the decision making process, especially from those directly involved; welcomes diverse opinions; open-minded (23)
- fiscally responsible; understands/has experience in school finance; seeks alternative/creative funding (21)
- understands and is actively involved in the legislative process at the local and state level (19)

- able to make a tough decision, follows through in a timely manner, and accept responsibility for that decision (18)
- highly visible and actively involved in the community (16)
- works well with other governmental and community agencies (15)
- has a positive track record in labor relations; treats all employees equally and fairly; realizes the value of the support staff (14)
- values and respects teachers (13)
- empowers principals; supports site-based decision making (12)
- approachable/available (11)
- ensures that discipline policies are implemented fairly and consistently throughout the district (10)
- will evaluate the substance abuse concerns at the high school and take necessary action if needed (10)
- is from outside of the district (9)
- has relevant/recent teaching experience (9)
- will mentor and encourage all persons to reach his/her potential; will mentor new leaders (9)
- is a strong leader; a strong person (9)
- believes that extracurricular activities should be "co" curricular activities, i.e., music; supports a strong athletic program (8)
- has a sense of humor (8)
- a Joe "clone" (7)
- able to deal with conflict in a positive and professional manner (7)
- visionary—with a focus (7)
- current on educational issues and research-will promote and support those which will benefit HTCS students (6)
- collaborative leader (6)
- will work well with the Board of Education (6)
- doesn't bend to pressure groups/individuals (6)
- promotes and supports technology (5)
- listens to parents; expects and encourages parental involvement in the schools (5)
- follows the chain of command and ensures that other do the same (4)
- is not ego/self-centered (4)
- understands the role of, and works well with the HTESA (4)
- returns phone calls promptly (4)
- previous experience as a superintendent (3)
- promotes/champion the positive aspects of HTCS (3)
- understands and supports elementary education (3)
- does not make change for change's sake (3)
- is professional at all times (2)

HOME TOWN COMMUNITY SCHOOLS
BOARD OF EDUCATION
SUPERINTENDENT PROFILE

Board members, after receiving input from employees, students, and community groups, have selected the following characteristics as having particular importance for candidates seeking to become the new Superintendent of Home Town Community Schools :

- A leader who demonstrates the highest degree of integrity, honesty, trustworthiness, consistency, and openness to all persons; has high moral and ethical standards; is professional at all times; is a good role model.
- A positive, energetic, organized, enthusiastic leader who is highly visible throughout the school system; truly likes kids and keeps kids first, always; visits classrooms/departments on a regular basis; knows what is going on; supports and regularly attends various school activities at all levels; known by all students, communicates with students on a regular basis, and seeks their input in decisions which directly affect them; seeks, values, promotes, and expects parental and citizen involvement in the schools; has a positive attitude and promotes the positive aspects of the district and our community as a whole.
- A leader who demonstrates exemplary communication skills with all persons; fosters an open line of effective communication with all employees, students, and throughout the community as a whole; seeks and values input in the decision making process, especially from all who are directly involved; actively seeks and values diverse opinions; able to make a decision, follows through in a timely manner, and then accept responsibility for that decision; does not bend to pressure groups/individuals; is capable of articulating, communicating, and supporting well-reasoned positions on important issues of the district.
- A leader who will make a commitment to Home Town Community Schools and stay a while; understands, appreciates, and values the uniqueness of our community; wants to live in our community; will be highly visible and actively involved in our community; supports and promotes collaborative relationships with other governmental and community agencies, as well as other school districts.
- A leader who is a people person; down-to-earth, common, kind, caring, compassionate, and will provide a positive work environment; a good listener; honest, up front, tells it like it is; not self-centered; works

effectively with all persons; has a sense of humor; approachable/available, and promotes an open-door policy; supports and promotes an environment of continuous improvement; fosters and practices a collaborative management style.

- A strong educational leader who is and will remain current on educational issues and research; has a strong curriculum/instruction background; keeps academic achievement and the needs of all students as the number one priority; supports and promotes professional development for all employees; open-minded, creative, and innovative in his/her approach to education; ensures that all educational programs are treated equally and fairly; supports and promotes those changes which would enhance the educational opportunities for Home Town Community Schools Students.

- A leader who has demonstrated experience in or has knowledge of all areas of the superintendency, including school finance, school law, and labor relations; is fiscally responsible; will actively seek alternative/additional funding and/or grants; understands the legislative process and is actively involved when necessary.

- A leader who believes in, supports, and promotes the "team" concept of school/family/community; is a team builder and participant; able and willing to delegate responsibility and holds all persons accountable in their respective positions; supports a strong administrative team; believes that principals are the educational leaders of their individual buildings; believes in and supports site based decision making; able to recognize, promote, and enhance the talents and expertise of students, employees, and citizens; treats all persons equally, fairly, and with respect and dignity; has a track record of positive labor relations, including a positive experience in negotiations; ensures that all policies/procedures are implemented fairly and consistently throughout the district; follows the chain of command and expects others to do the same; able to deal with conflict and sensitive issues in a positive and professional manner; works well with the Board of Education.

- A visionary leader who motivates, builds consensus, and in concert with the board, unites the employees and community around a shared and planned vision of the district's future and exercises sound judgment in leadership toward that future.

Reference # 13

MEMORANDUM

TO: All Home Town Community Schools Employees and Citizens
FROM: Consultant
RE: Superintendent Search
DATE: March 7, 20__

I would like to take this opportunity to thank you for the time and effort you put forth in attending the input sessions for the superintendent search. Your opinions and ideas are valued and greatly appreciated.

Attached is a copy of the superintendent profile which was adopted by the Board of Education at a meeting held on March 6, 20__. Copies of the brochure will be available at the superintendent's office by March 10, 20__, if you should desire to have your own copy.

Please refer to the calendar on the back of this memo for the remaining timelines regarding the superintendent search. The candidates to be interviewed will be determined by the Board of Education on April 27, 20_. The schedule of persons to be interviewed will be available to you on April 28, 20_. The interviews are open to the public and we welcome your attendance and appreciate your input.

If anyone has any questions, concerns, or comments, please leave a message with Susie at the superintendent's office, and I will get back to you as soon as possible.

Once again, thanks for your continued interest, and I hope to see you at the interviews.

Reference # 14

VERIFICATION STATEMENT
(Please read carefully and sign the statement below.)

The information in my application is true, correct, and complete to the best of my knowledge. I certify that I have answered all questions to the best of my ability, and I have not withheld any information that would unfavorably affect my application for employment. I acknowledge that any misrepresentation or omission of any fact in my application, resume, or any other materials, or during any interviews, may be the cause for my rejection from employment or may result in my dismissal if I am hired.

_____   _____
                Signature   *Date*

I request that my application file remain confidential pursuant to and in accordance with the state laws.

_____   _____
                Signature   Date

Applicant's File Must Include:

- A letter of application stating personal qualifications, experiences, and reasons for interest in the position.
- A completed official application form and current resume.
- The names of three persons who will serve as references and can be contacted. (Include name, title, and telephone numbers for both home and business and a cell phone number, if known.)
- A minimum of four current letters of recommendation.

Please Direct *All* Inquiries,
Applications and Supporting Materials To:

Company address
phone
fax
e-mail

DO NOT CONTACT THE DISTRICT OR BOARD MEMBERS DIRECTLY.

Reference # 15

BOARD MEMBER SUGGESTED GUIDELINE FOR REVIEWING CANDIDATE FILES

Some suggestions for review of individual candidate files are as follows (the grid with candidate names on it is for you to use in any way that may help you to compare candidates to one another):

1. The file, in general, is it:
    - organized
    - professional in appearance
    - complete information
    - application form itself
        - handwritten or typed
        - filled out completely
    - two questions at the end of the application—answered?

2. The letter of interest, is/does it:
    - well-written
    - address the district concerns and positives in any way
    - to the point without rambling
    - address *why* he/she wants the job

3. The resume, is it (or does it tell us):
    - easy to read
    - give educational background and experience in an organized manner
    - currently employed
    - any information (dates) omitted
    - articles written
    - honors received

4. Letters of recommendation:
    - current
    - from immediate supervisor
    - anything of a questionable nature

5. Some questions specific to our district needs (you might want to refer to the profile and make headings on the grid):
   - superintendent or central office experience
   - length of time in one place
   - ability to deal with conflict in a positive manner
   - understands school finance
   - any area *you* may want to emphasize
   - involvement in the community
   - excellent communication skills

6. Does this person seem to fit our needs?

If you have any questions, please feel free to call me.

Reference # 16

HOME TOWN COMMUNITY SCHOOLS
SUPERINTENDENT SEARCH
CANDIDATE LIST

Name	Position	District/State	Degree	Req. met
Brown, Susan	A/Supt	Big Pine/MI	PhD	Yes
Clay, Bill	Supt	Moby/GA	EdS	Yes
Downs, Jane	HSP	Oldtown/TX	MA+	No
.	.	.	.	.
.	.	.	.	.
.	.	.	.	.
.	.	.	.	.
.	.	.	.	.

HOME TOWN COMMUNITY SCHOOLS
BOARD OF EDUCATION
SUPERINTENDENT SEARCH
SPECIAL MEETING
APRIL 27, 20__

CLOSED SESSION TO REVIEW SPECIFIC CONTENTS OF THOSE
EMPLOYMENT APPLICATIONS WHERE APPLICANTS REQUESTED
CONFIDENTIALITY AND CLOSED SESSION.

OPEN SESSION
1. Select candidates to be interviewed   (action item)
2. Set dates and times for interviews   (action item)

April 19, 20__

Dear Board Members,

Enclosed are the files of all candidates who applied for the Home Town Community Schools superintendent position. The files must be kept together, as strict confidentiality is very important. No part of any file may be duplicated. Names of candidates must not be shared or discussed with any other person—only another board member. The lists are for you to use individually but are *not* to be shared with anyone other than board members. Once the selection of who is to be interviewed takes place, then the list of candidates must be destroyed before it gets into the hands of anyone other than board members.

I have included a list of suggestions on how to review the files and have made a grid with the names of candidates on it—for you to use in any way helpful to you. I have also included some notes on what you may want to use as headings for the columns.

The agenda for Thursday evening, April 27, 20__, is attached. Usually, we complete the entire process within three hours. It is an exhausting but exciting activity. We have some excellent candidates. I think you will be very pleased with what you see.

If anyone has any questions, please feel free to call me on the cellular (XXX XXX XXXX) and if I don't happen to answer, please leave a message, and I'll get right back to you.

See you on April 27th!

Consultant's Signature

CANDIDATE: _____ BOARD MEMBER_____

HOME TOWN COMMUNITY SCHOOLS
SUPERINTENDENT SEARCH
INTERVIEW QUESTIONS

1. WHY DO YOU WANT TO LEAVE YOUR CURRENT POSITION TO BECOME THE SUPERINTENDENT OF HOME TOWN COMMUNITY SCHOOLS?

   WHAT DID YOU DO TO PREPARE YOURSELF SPECIFICALLY FOR THIS INTERVIEW?

2. WHAT WAS YOUR MOST UNIQUE OR INNOVATIVE ACCOMPLISHMENT IN YOUR PRESENT POSITION?

3. HOW WOULD YOU GO ABOUT BUILDING A TEAM ATMOSPHERE AMONG THE EMPLOYEES, COMMUNITY, AND BOARD?

4. HOW CAN WE PROVIDE DIVERSE AND EFFECTIVELY STIMULATING EDUCATIONAL OPPORTUNITIES FOR STUDENTS AT THE HIGHEST ACHIEVEMENT LEVELS, ESPECIALLY IN THE EARLY GRADES?

   HOW DO YOU ENSURE THAT ALL STUDENTS ARE EDUCATIONALLY CHALLENGED?

5. WHAT IS YOUR PHILOSOPHY REGARDING PROFESSIONAL DEVELOPMENT FOR ALL EMPLOYEES, AND HOW DO YOU CONTINUE YOUR OWN PROFESSIONAL GROWTH?

6. PLEASE GIVE US ONE EXAMPLE OF HOW YOU HAVE USED YOUR DECISION-MAKING SKILLS TO SOLVE A PROBLEM WITHIN YOUR CURRENT DISTRICT.

   WHAT ROLE DO ADMINISTRATORS HAVE IN THE DECISION-MAKING PROCESS?

7. DESCRIBE THE BOARD/SUPERINTENDENT RELATIONSHIP YOU WOULD LIKE TO SEE AND TELL US HOW YOU WOULD PROMOTE THAT RELATIONSHIP.

    WHAT WOULD YOUR CURRENT BOARD SAY ABOUT YOU?

8. PLEASE PROVIDE US WITH ONE EXAMPLE OF HOW YOU HAVE ENCOURAGED AND BEEN SUCCESSFUL IN GETTING PARENTS AND COMMUNITY MEMBERS INVOLVED IN THE SCHOOLS.

9. WHAT DO YOU THINK MIGHT BE NECESSARY TO FACILITATE EFFICIENT USE OF TECHNOLOGY ENHANCED TEACHING AND LEARNING IN HOME TOWN COMMUNITY SCHOOLS?

5:50
7:20   (1/3)

8:50

10. WHAT WOULD YOUR PROCESS BE IN MAKING CHANGES IN ESTABLISHED PROGRAMS AND PROCEDURES?

11. WHAT HAS BEEN ONE OF YOUR FUNNIEST OR MOST EMBARRASSING MOMENTS AS A SUPERINTENDENT/ADMINISTRATOR?

12. WHAT OPTIONS FOR ALTERNATIVE EDUCATION CAN BE ACTIVATED IN HOME TOWN COMMUNITY SCHOOLS WITH THE LIMITED FUNDS AND FLEXIBILITY OF STATE-IMPOSED CURRICULUM?

13. HOW WOULD YOU BUILD TRUST AND ENCOURAGE PERSONS WITH DIFFERING VIEWPOINTS TO BE HEARD?

14. WITHIN THE ENTIRE SPECTRUM OF THE CURRICULUM, WHERE DO THE ARTS AND EXTRACURRICULAR PROGRAMS FIT IN?

15. WHAT IS YOUR DEFINITION OF COMMON SENSE?

    PLEASE GIVE US ONE EXAMPLE OF HOW YOU HAVE USED COMMON SENSE IN YOUR DISTRICT.

16. IF OUR DISTRICT WOULD RECEIVE A WINDFALL OF ONE MILLION DOLLARS, WHAT WOULD YOU RECOMMEND WE DO WITH IT?

17. IF YOU HAD TO MAKE CUTS IN THE BUDGET DUE TO DECLINING RESOURCES OR ECONOMIC EMERGENCIES, HOW WOULD YOU DETERMINE PRIORITIES IN ORDER TO RECOMMEND BUDGET REDUCTIONS TO THE BOARD?

18. WHAT ALTERNATIVE FUNDING WOULD YOU SEEK FOR OUR DISTRICT?

6:10
7:40 (2/3)

11:10

19. PLEASE GIVE US SPECIFIC EXAMPLES OF HOW YOU WOULD PLAN TO BE VISIBLE IN DISTRICT BUILDINGS, AT SCHOOL ACTIVITIES, AND IN THE COMMUNITY AS A WHOLE.

20. WHAT THREE ISSUES DO YOU SEE HOME TOWN COMMUNITY SCHOOLS FACING IN THE NEXT THREE YEARS?

21. WHAT PROCESS DO YOU USE TO HOLD PERSONS ACCOUNTABLE?

22. ON YOUR PRIORITY LIST, WHERE DOES THE MAINTENANCE OF FACILITIES RANK AND PLEASE TELL US WHY.

23. WHAT IS YOUR PHILOSOPHY REGARDING LABOR RELATIONS?

WHAT THREE INDEPENDENT WORDS WOULD YOUR EMPLOYEES USE IN DESCRIBING YOUR WORKING RELATIONSHIP WITH THEM?

24. WHAT TECHNIQUES WOULD YOU USE TO LET THE EMPLOYEES AND COMMUNITY KNOW YOU ARE WILLING TO HEAR FROM THEM REGARDING THEIR CONCERNS ABOUT THE DISTRICT?

25. HOW WOULD YOU PLAN TO SUPPORT COLLABORATIVE RELATIONSHIPS WITH OTHER DISTRICTS, THE CITY, TOWNSHIPS, THE BUSINESS COMMUNITY, ETC?

WHAT DO YOU SEE AS YOUR RESPONSIBILITY IN THE POLITICAL ARENA AS IT RELATES TO THE LOCAL AND STATE LEVEL?

26. WHAT SPECIFIC IDEAS DO YOU HAVE TO PROMOTE THE POSITIVE ASPECTS OF THE DISTRICT?

27. IF I WALKED INTO THE LOCAL COFFEE SHOP AND ASKED FOR AN EVALUATION OF YOUR JOB PERFORMANCE, WHAT WOULD I HEAR?

28. WHAT ARE TWO STRENGTHS YOU FEEL YOU HAVE WHICH WILL GREATLY BENEFIT HOME TOWN COMMUNITY SCHOOLS?

29. IS THERE ANYTHING ELSE YOU WOULD LIKE US TO KNOW ABOUT YOU?

6:25
7:55 (3/3)

9:25

30. WHAT QUESTIONS DO YOU HAVE FOR US?

THEN . . .

QUESTIONS FROM 3″ X 5″ CARDS
(HOW MANY YOU ASK WILL DEPEND UPON THE TIME REMAINING)

6:43
8:13 2-3 MINUTES TO CLOSING

9:43

31. DO YOU HAVE A CLOSING STATEMENT?

NOTES . . .

STRENGTHS

WHAT I WANT TO KNOW MORE ABOUT . . .

Reference # 20
Superintendent Profile

Board members, after receiving input from employees, students, and community groups, have selected the following characteristics as having particular importance for candidates seeking to become the new Superintendent of Home Town Community Schools:

o   A leader who demonstrates the highest degree of integrity, honesty, trustworthiness, consistency, and openness to all persons; has high moral and ethical standards; is professional at all times; is a good role model.

o   A positive, energetic, organized, enthusiastic leader who is highly visible throughout the school system; truly likes kids and keeps kids first, always; visits classrooms/departments on a regular basis; knows what is going on; supports and regularly attends various school activities at all levels; known by all students, communicates with students on a regular basis, and seeks their input in decisions which directly affect them; seeks, values, promotes, and expects parental and citizen involvement in the schools; has a positive attitude and promotes the positive aspects of the district and our community as a whole.

o   A leader who demonstrates exemplary communication skills with all persons; fosters an open line of effective communication with all employees, students, and throughout the community as a whole; seeks and values input in the decision-making process, especially from all who are directly involved; actively seeks and values diverse opinions; able to make a decision, follow through in a timely manner, and then accept responsibility for that decision; does not bend to pressure groups/individuals; is capable of articulating, communicating, and supporting well-reasoned positions on important issues of the district.

o   A leader who will make a commitment to Home Town Community Schools and stay a while; understands, appreciates, and values the uniqueness of our community; wants to live in our community; will be highly visible and actively involved in our community; supports and promotes collaborative relationships with other governmental and community agencies, as well as other school districts.

o   A leader who is a people person; down-to-earth, common, kind, caring, compassionate, and will provide a positive work environment; a good listener; honest, up front, tells it like it is; not self-centered; works effectively with all persons; has a sense of humor; approachable/available, and promotes an open door policy; supports and promotes an environment of continuous improvement; fosters and practices a collaborative management style.

o A strong educational leader who is and will remain current on educational issues and research; has a strong curriculum/instruction background; keeps academic achievement and the needs of all students as the number one priority; supports and promotes professional development for all employees; understands and promotes the effective use of technology in education; open-minded, creative, and innovative in his/her approach to education; ensures that all educational programs are treated equally and fairly; supports and promotes those changes which would enhance the educational opportunities for Home Town Community Schools Students.

o A leader who has demonstrated experience in or has knowledge of all areas of the superintendency, including school finance, school law and labor relations; is fiscally responsible; will actively seek alternative/additional funding and/or grants; understands the legislative process and is actively involved when necessary.

o A leader who believes in, supports, and promotes the "team" concept of school/family/community; is a team builder and participant; able and willing to delegate responsibility and holds all persons accountable in their respective positions; supports a strong administrative team; believes that principals are the educational leaders of their individual buildings; believes in and supports site based decision making; able to recognize, promote, and enhance the talents and expertise of students, employees, and citizens; treats all persons equally and fairly, with respect and dignity; has a track record of positive labor relations, including a positive experience in negotiations; ensures that all policies/procedures are implemented fairly and consistently throughout the district; follows the chain of command and expects others to do the same; able to deal with conflict and sensitive issues in a positive and professional manner; works well with the Board of Education.

o A visionary leader who motivates, builds consensus, and in concert with the board, unites the employees and community around a shared and planned vision of the district's future.

Reference # 21

HOME TOWN COMMUNITY SCHOOLS
SUPERINTENDENT SEARCH
INTERVIEW RATING SHEET

Rating scale: 1-5
Highest rating: 5

CANDIDATE_____

BOARD MEMBER_____

I. PERSONAL CHARACTERISTICS:

1. Communication skills   ☐☐☐☐☐
2. Appearance   ☐☐☐☐☐
3. Composure   ☐☐☐☐☐

II. ABILITY TO:

1. Express ideas clearly   ☐☐☐☐☐
2. Listen and respond effectively   ☐☐☐☐☐
3. Visualize future needs   ☐☐☐☐☐
4. Build a strong school "team"   ☐☐☐☐☐

III. RESPONSES TO QUESTIONS:

1. Why Home Town Community Schools   ☐☐☐☐☐
2. Accomplishments   ☐☐☐☐☐
3. Team builder   ☐☐☐☐☐
4. Academics   ☐☐☐☐☐
5. Professional development   ☐☐☐☐☐
6. Problem solving   ☐☐☐☐☐
7. Board/Supt relations   ☐☐☐☐☐
8. Parent/community involvement   ☐☐☐☐☐
9. Technology   ☐☐☐☐☐
10. Making changes   ☐☐☐☐☐
11. Sense of humor   ☐☐☐☐☐
12. Alternative education   ☐☐☐☐☐
13. Build trust   ☐☐☐☐☐
14. Arts/extracurricular   ☐☐☐☐☐

15. Common sense ☐☐☐☐☐
16. Windfall ☐☐☐☐☐
17. Budget cuts ☐☐☐☐☐
18. Alternative funding ☐☐☐☐☐
19. Visibility ☐☐☐☐☐
20. Three future issues ☐☐☐☐☐
21. Accountability ☐☐☐☐☐
22. Building/grounds maintenance ☐☐☐☐☐
23. Labor relations ☐☐☐☐☐
24. Employee/community communications ☐☐☐☐☐
25. Collaborative relationships ☐☐☐☐☐
26. Provide positive supports ☐☐☐☐☐
27. Coffee shop, etc. ☐☐☐☐☐

Reference #22

NAME_____

PHONE_____

CANDIDATE QUESTIONS (CONSULTANT)

1. Briefly indicate the reasons you are seeking this particular position. Have you visited the district?
2. Based on what you know and have been told about this position, what do you believe is your strongest qualification?
3. How would you build strong community relationships?
4. Describe any experience you have had in K-12 curriculum.
5. What are your career goals? How long would you plan to stay in the district?
6. What experience have you had in school finance?
7. What has been the greatest challenge you faced in your current leadership role, and how did you deal with it?
8. How visible would you plan to be throughout the district?
9. If you were selected for this position, in what area would you need and expect the most help from the school board?
10. Describe your procedure for building a positive team atmosphere with the administrators, staff, students, community.
11. Describe your leadership style.
12. Describe how you would assess the district needs in the area of internal and external communications.
13. What procedures would you use to build a positive team relationship with the school board?
14. Would you plan to live in the district?
15. Salary, benefits, etc?
16. Family?
17. Other applications out?
18. How long is your current contract? Release from current contract a problem?
19. What three individual words—after one year—would describe your performance?
20. Is there anything in your background which would be an embarrassment to the board or me, should it be found out after your name is published?

Reference # 23

April 12, 20__

Candidate name/address

Dear,

On behalf of the Board of Education, I would like to thank you for your interest in the Home Town Community Schools superintendent position.

At a special board meeting on April 11, 20__, the Board of Education reviewed the files of each candidate. After much deliberation over the outstanding list of candidates, the board selected the persons to interview.

Unfortunately, you were not one of the persons selected to be interviewed. Therefore, the Board does not plan to continue your candidacy.

Once again, thank you for your interest in the Home Town Community Schools, and we wish you much success as you pursue a change in your current position.

Sincerely,

Consultant's Signature

Reference # 24

To: All Home Town Community Schools Employees and Citizens
From: Consultant-Company
Re: Superintendent Candidates
Date: April 28, 20__

The Home Town Board of Education, at a special board meeting held on April 27, 20__, selected the following persons as candidates for superintendent . . .

Name	Position	Interview Date/Time
Jane Brown	A/Supt/Big Pine/MI	May 1-5:30 p.m.
.	.	.
.	.	.
.	.	.
.	.	.
.	.	.

All interviews are scheduled to be held in the Media Center at the high school. Please plan to attend, ask the candidates questions if you so desire, and give your input to the board members between and/or after the interview sessions.

A copy of the above candidates' files are available at the superintendent's office for your review.

Anyone who would desire to attend the site visits with the Board of Education is asked to put his/her request in writing to Joe Smith, Board President, and send it directly to him at the superintendent's office no later than noon on Monday, May 1, 20__. All persons desiring to attend the site visits must attend *all* of the interviews.

Looking forward to seeing you at the interviews!

HOME TOWN COMMUNITY SCHOOLS
BOARD OF EDUCATION
SUPERINTENDENT SEARCH
SPECIAL MEETING
APRIL 27, 20__

INTERVIEW WORKSHOP

1. Interview

   What to look for:
   • Physical appearance
   • Personality
   • Self-confidence
   • Eye contact—one, all, none
   • Answers questions? Avoidance?
   • Sense of humor
   • Handshake

2. Before interview—meet informally

3. Board President Guidelines

4. Review actual questions

5. Rating sheet

6. 3″ X 5″ cards

7. Room setup

8. Other Items

Home Visit
   a. when
   b. team

Reference # 26

SAMPLES OF ANSWERS TO QUESTIONS

QUESTION: WHY DO YOU WANT TO LEAVE YOUR CURRENT POSITION TO BECOME THE SUPERINTENDENT OF HOME TOWN COMMUNITY SCHOOLS?

GOOD ANSWER: During my research of your district, I have found that my talents and expertise seem to fit your profile and stated needs. Your district is also a larger district located in an area to which my family and I desire to relocate.

BAD ANSWER: I have been released from my current position and need a job.

AROUND THE QUESTION ANSWER: I have talked to some friends of mine and they say this is a good district and I like to fish. I noted you have many lakes nearby.

NOTE: Answers should be direct and indicate in various ways that the candidate has done his/her research and desires to be the next superintendent.

Reference # 27

CANDIDATE: _____ BOARD MEMBER_____

HOME TOWN COMMUNITY SCHOOLS
SUPERINTENDENT SEARCH
INTERVIEW QUESTIONS

SUE 1. WHY DO YOU WANT TO LEAVE YOUR CURRENT POSITION TO BECOME THE SUPERINTENDENT OF HOME TOWN COMMUNITY SCHOOLS?

WHAT DID YOU DO TO PREPARE YOURSELF SPECIFICALLY FOR THIS INTERVIEW?

JANE 2. WHAT WAS YOUR MOST UNIQUE OR INNOVATIVE ACCOMPLISHMENT IN YOUR PRESENT POSITION?

BOB 3. HOW WOULD YOU GO ABOUT BUILDING A TEAM ATMOSPHERE AMONG THE EMPLOYEES, COMMUNITY, AND BOARD?

SALLY 4. HOW CAN WE PROVIDE DIVERSE AND EFFECTIVELY STIMULATING EDUCATIONAL OPPORTUNITIES FOR STUDENTS AT THE HIGHEST ACHIEVEMENT LEVELS, ESPECIALLY IN THE EARLY GRADES?

HOW DO YOU ENSURE THAT ALL STUDENTS ARE EDUCATIONALLY CHALLENGED?

RAY 5. WHAT IS YOUR PHILOSOPHY REGARDING PROFESSIONAL DEVELOPMENT FOR ALL EMPLOYEES, AND HOW DO YOU CONTINUE YOUR OWN PROFESSIONAL GROWTH?

JOE 6. PLEASE GIVE US ONE EXAMPLE OF HOW YOU HAVE USED YOUR DECISION-MAKING SKILLS TO SOLVE A PROBLEM WITHIN YOUR CURRENT DISTRICT.

WHAT ROLE DO ADMINISTRATORS HAVE IN THE DECISION-MAKING PROCESS?

AL   7. DESCRIBE THE BOARD/SUPERINTENDENT RELATIONSHIP YOU WOULD LIKE TO SEE AND TELL US HOW YOU WOULD PROMOTE THAT RELATIONSHIP.

        WHAT WOULD YOUR CURRENT BOARD SAY ABOUT YOU?

SALLY 8. PLEASE PROVIDE US WITH ONE EXAMPLE OF HOW YOU HAVE ENCOURAGED AND BEEN SUCCESSFUL IN GETTING PARENTS AND COMMUNITY MEMBERS INVOLVED IN THE SCHOOLS.

SUE   9. HOW DO COMPONENTS OF SCHOOLNET SERVE THE TEACHER/ STUDENT/PARENT TECHNOLOGY INTERFACE, AND WHAT ELSE MIGHT BE NECESSARY TO FACILITATE EFFICIENT USE OF TECHNOLOGY ENHANCED TEACHING AND LEARNING IN HOME TOWN COMMUNITY SCHOOLS?

5:50
7:20 (1/3)

8:50

BOB   10. WHAT WOULD YOUR PROCESS BE IN MAKING CHANGES IN ESTABLISHED PROGRAMS AND PROCEDURES?

JANE   11. WHAT HAS BEEN ONE OF YOUR FUNNIEST OR MOST EMBARRASSING MOMENTS AS A SUPERINTENDENT/ADMIN?

RAY   12. WHAT OPTIONS FOR ALTERNATIVE EDUCATION CAN BE ACTIVATED IN HOME TOWN COMMUNITY SCHOOLS, WITH THE LIMITED FUNDS AND FLEXIBILITY OF STATE IMPOSED CURRICULUM?

AL   13. HOW WOULD YOU BUILD TRUST AND ENCOURAGE PERSONS WITH DIFFERING VIEWPOINTS TO BE HEARD?

JOE   14. WITHIN THE ENTIRE SPECTRUM OF THE CURRICULUM, WHERE DO THE ARTS AND EXTRACURRICULAR PROGRAMS FIT IN?

BOB   15. WHAT IS YOUR DEFINITION OF COMMON SENSE?

        PLEASE GIVE US ONE EXAMPLE OF HOW YOU HAVE USED COMMON SENSE IN YOUR DISTRICT.

JANE 16. IF OUR DISTRICT WOULD RECEIVE A WINDFALL OF ONE MILLION DOLLARS, WHAT WOULD YOU RECOMMEND WE DO WITH IT?

SALLY 17. IF YOU HAD TO MAKE CUTS IN THE BUDGET DUE TO DECLINING RESOURCES OR ECONOMIC EMERGENCIES, HOW WOULD YOU DETERMINE PRIORITIES IN ORDER TO RECOMMEND BUDGET REDUCTIONS TO THE BOARD?

SUE 18. WHAT ALTERNATIVE FUNDING WOULD YOU SEEK FOR OUR DISTRICT?

6:10
7:40 (2/3)

9:10

AL 19. PLEASE GIVE US SPECIFIC EXAMPLES OF HOW YOU WOULD PLAN TO BE VISIBLE IN DISTRICT BUILDINGS, AT SCHOOL ACTIVITIES, AND IN THE COMMUNITY AS A WHOLE.

BOB 20. WHAT THREE ISSUES DO YOU SEE HOME TOWN COMMUNITY SCHOOLS FACING IN THE NEXT THREE YEARS?

JOE 21. WHAT PROCESS DO YOU USE TO HOLD PERSONS ACCOUNTABLE?

JANE 22. ON YOUR PRIORITY LIST, WHERE DOES THE MAINTENANCE OF FACILITIES RANK AND PLEASE TELL US WHY.

RAY 23. WHAT IS YOUR PHILOSOPHY REGARDING LABOR RELATIONS?

WHAT THREE INDEPENDENT WORDS WOULD YOUR EMPLOYEES USE IN DESCRIBING YOUR WORKING RELATIONSHIP WITH THEM?

SUE 24. WHAT TECHNIQUES WOULD YOU USE TO LET THE EMPLOYEES AND COMMUNITY KNOW YOU ARE WILLING TO HEAR FROM THEM REGARDING THEIR CONCERNS ABOUT THE DISTRICT?

RAY 25. HOW WOULD YOU PLAN TO SUPPORT COLLABORATIVE RELATIONSHIPS WITH OTHER DISTRICTS, THE CITY, TOWNSHIPS, THE BUSINESS COMMUNITY, ETC.?

WHAT DO YOU SEE AS YOUR RESPONSIBILITY IN THE POLITICAL ARENA AS IT RELATES TO THE LOCAL AND STATE LEVEL?

JOE 26. WHAT SPECIFIC IDEAS DO YOU HAVE TO PROMOTE THE POSITIVE ASPECTS OF THE DISTRICT?

AL 27. IF I WALKED INTO THE LOCAL COFFEE SHOP AND ASKED FOR AN EVALUATION OF YOUR JOB PERFORMANCE, WHAT WOULD I HEAR?

SALLY 28. WHAT ARE TWO STRENGTHS YOU FEEL YOU HAVE WHICH WILL GREATLY BENEFIT HOME TOWN COMMUNITY SCHOOLS?

SUE 29. IS THERE ANYTHING ELSE YOU WOULD LIKE US TO KNOW ABOUT YOU?

6:25
7:55 (3/3)

9:25

SUE 30. WHAT QUESTIONS DO YOU HAVE FOR US?

THEN . . .

***QUESTIONS FROM 3″ X 5″ CARDS ***(HOW MANY YOU ASK WILL DEPEND UPON THE TIME REMAINING)

6:43
8:13 2-3 MINUTES TO CLOSING

9:43

SUE 31. DO YOU HAVE A CLOSING STATEMENT?

NOTES . . .

STRENGTHS . . .

WHAT I WANT TO KNOW MORE ABOUT . . .

Reference # 28

HOME TOWN COMMUNITY SCHOOLS
SUPERINTENDENT SEARCH
INTERVIEW RATING SHEET

Rating scale: 1-5
Highest rating: 5

CANDIDATE_____

BOARD MEMBER_____

I. PERSONAL CHARACTERISTICS:

   1. Communication skills   ☐☐☐☐☐
   2. Appearance   ☐☐☐☐☐
   3. Composure   ☐☐☐☐☐

II. ABILITY TO:

   1. Express ideas clearly   ☐☐☐☐☐
   2. Listen and respond effectively   ☐☐☐☐☐
   3. Visualize future needs   ☐☐☐☐☐
   4. Build a strong school "team"   ☐☐☐☐☐

III. RESPONSES TO QUESTIONS:

   1. Why Home Town Community Schools   ☐☐☐☐☐
   2. Accomplishments   ☐☐☐☐☐
   3. Team builder   ☐☐☐☐☐
   4. Academics   ☐☐☐☐☐
   5. Professional development   ☐☐☐☐☐
   6. Problem solving   ☐☐☐☐☐
   7. Board/Supt relations   ☐☐☐☐☐
   8. Parent/community involvement   ☐☐☐☐☐
   9. Technology   ☐☐☐☐☐
   10. Making changes   ☐☐☐☐☐
   11. Sense of humor   ☐☐☐☐☐
   12. Alternative education   ☐☐☐☐☐
   13. Build trust   ☐☐☐☐☐

14. Arts/extra curricular ☐☐☐☐☐
15. Common sense ☐☐☐☐☐
16. Windfall ☐☐☐☐☐
17. Budget cuts ☐☐☐☐☐
18. Alternative funding ☐☐☐☐☐
19. Visibility ☐☐☐☐☐
20. Three future issues ☐☐☐☐☐
21. Accountability ☐☐☐☐☐
22. Building/grounds maintenance ☐☐☐☐☐
23. Labor relations ☐☐☐☐☐
24. Employee/community communications ☐☐☐☐☐
25. Collaborative relationships ☐☐☐☐☐
26. Promote positive aspects ☐☐☐☐☐
27. Coffee shop, etc. ☐☐☐☐☐

Reference # 29

HOME TOWN COMMUNITY SCHOOLS
SUPERINTENDENT INTERVIEW
GUIDELINE FOR CHAIRPERSON

The following guidelines are for your use during the interview:

At the beginning of each interview . . .
. . . Indicate the time frame to the candidate.
. . . Indicate to the audience that if anyone has a question or questions for the candidate please write them on a 3″ X 5″ card available on the table (indicate where) and the consultant will collect the questions near the end of each interview.

At the end of the interview . . .

. . . Thank the candidate for his/her interest in our schools.

QUESTIONS MAY NOT BE ASKED ABOUT:

1. Religion

2. Age

3. Race or national origin

4. Marital or family status

5. Gender-oriented issues (This includes questions to women relative to whether or not family matters such as childhood or household care problems might interfere with responsibilities.)

6. Sexual preference

7. Political preference or activity

April 28, 200_

Rob Fields
123 Park Avenue
Big River, MI 58888

Dear Rob,

This letter is to confirm your scheduled interview with the Home Town Board of Education on Wednesday, May 3, 20__, at 5:30 p.m. in the Media Center at Home Town High School, located at 456 River Street, in Home Town. You are asked to arrive fifteen minutes early for the purpose of meeting board members and other interested individuals on an informal basis prior to the formal interview. The interview is scheduled for a maximum time of one hour and fifteen minutes.

You are encouraged to take time to research the district and tour the buildings prior to the interview. Please call Susie, Superintendent's Secretary, at xxx-xxx-xxxx, to schedule an appointment with persons you wish to see, plan a tour the district, and request specific materials you wish to review during your visit. The district will not be sending any information/materials to you.

Additional information for you . . .

1. Members of the audience who desire to ask the candidate specific questions will be asked to write their questions on a 3″ X 5″ card, and I will collect the questions near the end of each interview. I will review the question(s) and give the card to the board president at the conclusion of the board's scheduled questions. Depending upon the time remaining, the board president will decide which and how many questions will be used.

2. During the interview, board members may be making notations regarding your answers on their prepared list of questions.

3. Please plan to have no more than two prepared questions for the Board of Education and a closing statement no longer than one minute in length.

4. Please be reminded that there are no reimbursements for your expenses to participate in this initial interview. You are encouraged to bring your spouse and/or family with you to the interview.

5. You will be contacted late Wednesday night, May 3, 20__, to update you on the status of your candidacy.

If you have any questions or concerns regarding your interview, please feel free to call me at xxx-xxx-xxxx.

Looking forward to seeing you at the interview!

                                        Sincerely,

                                        Consultant's signature

INTERVIEW SETUP

ITEMS NEEDED:

Pencils
3″ X 5″ Cards
Water for Board Members and Candidate
Board Nameplates
Copies of Candidate Bios
Copies of Interview Schedule
Extra Brochures
Video and Monitors
Videotape (individual)
Microphones (especially for candidate)
Snacks, Coffee, Punch, etc.

ROOM SETUP:

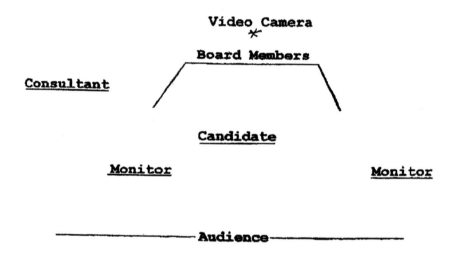

Table with schedules, pencils, 3″ X 5″ cards, candidate bios

**Entrance to room should be behind or at the side of the audience.

Reference # 32

HOME TOWN COMMUNITY SCHOOLS
SUPERINTENDENT SEARCH
SELECTION OF FINALISTS
MAY 3, 20__

1. Three areas of referral to help make your decisions . . .

   a. your individual notes
   b. rating sheets
   c. input from audience, etc.

2. Board/audience discussion of strengths and "What I'd like to know more about" each candidate

MOTION: Naming of finalists

3. Visit to home towns . . .

   a. which candidates
   b. board team
   c. dates of visits

MOTION: Board Team and dates

4. Team report date: MAY 11, 20__

5. Appointment of Superintendent: MAY 11, 20__

6. Contract Committee

Reference # 33

May 4, 200_

Dear Board Members and Board Committee Members,

Enclosed please find the following materials:

1. Letter regarding visit guidelines
2. List of materials to take with you
3. Suggested list of persons to see on visit
4. Guidelines sent to each candidate
5. Information regarding each candidate
   - letter sent to each candidate
   - file material on each candidate
   - suggested and specific questions for each candidate
   - information sent from each candidate
6. Guideline on site visit report
7. Agenda for the board meeting
8. Motion

HAVE A GREAT TIME!!!

Consultant's Signature

May 4, 20__

Dear Board Members and Board Committee Members,

Enclosed are suggested basic questions for each candidate. Please feel free to use all or some of the suggested questions—do whatever best suits your way of finding out everything you can about the candidate. The site visit is done for three reasons: (1) validate what is in the file, (2) validate what the candidate said at the interview, and (3) leave no stone unturned. Some of you will desire to follow the schedule the candidate will have put together (guidelines sent to candidates included with this memo), and the rest of you will want to wear your tennis shoes—you should go to every coffee shop, barber shop, beauty shop, hardware store, etc., and ask many questions about the candidate. Also, don't forget to talk with the custodians, secretaries, food service, bus drivers, etc. The only thing you may not do is interrupt teachers who are teaching in the classrooms. Remember, if you only hear all good things about a candidate, it usually has a hidden meaning. You should always find some folks who don't particularly like the candidate because of some reason or another. Anyone who has ever made a decision has made someone unhappy somewhere. What we want to know is how the unhappy person was treated when he or she had a disagreement with the candidate.

I've also included the fax which was sent to each candidate. Each candidate will review the visit schedule with you during your initial meeting which should include the entire team. After the initial meeting, the group should decide who stays with the schedules and who scatters. The last hour of the visit should bring all team members back together to meet with the candidate to clarify or ask any further questions.

Sometime during the day, the board president and another board member should meet with the candidate and ask if he/she will come to the district for the base salary as advertised. I always suggest that board members (one or two or three at the same time) should plan to meet with the candidate sometime during the day, on an individual basis and ask any questions you desire. Also, the board president should have the candidate sign the criminal check/ professional conduct release (whatever forms are used by your district).

The reports to the community should include an overview of your schedule for the day and a summary of comments. The reports don't have to be long—just sufficient enough to give an overall summary. I've enclosed a guideline.

I've also included with this memo the agenda for the Thursday (April 11, 20__) board meeting. I would expect this portion of the meeting to last about an hour.

Have a *great* time on your visits, and I'll be in touch with the board president after each visit. See you all on May 11th!

Consultant's Signature

MATERIALS TO TAKE WITH YOU TO THE SITE VISIT . . .

1. Packet sent by consultant

2. Duplicated material out of candidate information book

3. Materials faxed to district by candidate

4. Criminal check release (2)
(board president obtains candidate's signature)

5. Your notes taken during interview

6. Extra paper to write on

7. Copy of brochure (for reference to profile)

NOTE: POSTING OF THE MEETING(S) SHOULD BE FAXED OR EMAILED TO CANDIDATE TO BE POSTED WITHIN THE REQUIRED TIME FRAME.

PERSONS TO SEE/TALK WITH ON SITE VISIT:

- Administrators/central office/building
- Current supervisor/board members
- Association members—support and certified
- Students
- PTA/Boosters Clubs
- Police Chief
- City Council members
- Chamber of Commerce member/Rotary/Lions. etc.
- Persons on the street/coffee shops
- Business owners
- Ministers

May 4, 20__

Rob Fields
123 Park Avenue
Big River, MI 58888

Dear Rob,

The Home Town Board of Education desires to continue your candidacy for its superintendent of schools. Therefore, board members, employees, and community members will visit your place of employment on Wednesday, May 8, 20__.

Names of the persons planning to visit your district are included with this letter. They plan to arrive at 9:00 a.m. and will be in the district until approximately 3:00 p.m. The visit should begin and end with an approximate one-half-hour meeting with you.

It is important that the visitors have the opportunity to meet with a broad, cross-section of employees and community representatives—some of whom do not necessarily support everything you have done. Examples include the following:

- Administrators/Central Office/Principals
- Board members
- Association members—support and certified
- Students
- PTA/Booster Clubs
- Police Chief/Fire Chief
- Ministerial Association
- Chamber of Commerce member/Rotary/Lions, etc.

Please provide the committee with options of coffee shops or restaurants for their convenience. A tentative schedule for the day, along with a map to the place where they will meet you, should be faxed to Susie, Superintendent's Secretary, by 10:00 a.m. on Friday, May 5, 20__. Her fax number is xxx-xxx-xxxx.

We thank you for your continued interest in Home Town Community Schools and if you have any questions, please feel free to call me at xxx-xxx-xxxx.

Consultant's Signature

TO SUPERINTENDENT CANDIDATES:

SUGGESTIONS FOR SCHEDULING A VISIT TO YOUR DISTRICT . . .

First half hour with entire group
Review schedule for the day
Determine lunch arrangements (candidate is not expected to pick up the costs)

Fifteen-minute break

Next half hour—meeting with first home group

Fifteen-minute break

Next half hour—meeting with second home group

Fifteen—minute break

Next half hour—meeting with third home group

One hour and forty-five minutes—lunch break

Next half hour—meeting with fourth home group

Fifteen-minute break

Meeting with entire group (one-half hour)

Group meets without candidate for one-half hour—candidate should be somewhere near if any further questions come up.

End of visit—candidate returns to group to thank them for coming.

NOTES:

The entire visit is to be six hours. Candidate should schedule two groups to run simultaneously (group 1 and 2 or A and B). I would suggest that groups be of like positions—teachers with teachers, bus drivers with bus drivers, etc. In scheduling this way, the candidate will bring together eight different groups of people throughout the day. Sometime during the day, board members should plan to meet individually or in groups of two or three with the candidate—purpose is to get to know the candidate better. Also, the board president will need to obtain the permission for a criminal check—state law and the district will use their own form for candidate to sign.

Candidate should have an ID (or name tags) for all visitors so they will be readily identified by employees, students, and members of the community.

Suggested list of materials to have ready for review:

- any portfolio material
- district communications to the public
- district communications to employees
- typical board packet for a board meeting
- communications (examples) to the board
- any written materials which demonstrate your leadership role or specific philosophies
- board minutes
- newspaper articles
- anything you would like to share to promote *you and what you have done and what you believe in*

Reference # 35

GUIDELINE FOR REPORT ON SITE VISIT

1. The total report on all visits should last no longer than one hour.

2. The report should be a summary of the answers to the questions asked and include how the candidate fits the district profile, highlight strengths and answer specific questions on each individual candidate. The report may be narrative or outlined, whichever way the committee/reporter desires.

3. Verbal report may be given by one or more members of the total team (often main report is given by a non-board member with all team members adding their own comment(s) at the end of the report.

4. Remember to highlight the *strengths* and how the candidate fits the profile.

5. No written report needs to, nor should be, distributed.

NOTE: The report is a summary of your findings during the visit, not a committee recommendation to the Board of Education. You may add your personal comments regarding which person you would like to see the board offer a contract, keeping in mind that only the members of the board make the decision.

Reference # 36 A/B

MOTION TO SELECT SUPERINTENDENT: (A)

Board Member: I hereby make a motion that we offer a contract for the position of superintendent to _____for a period of *three years, at a base salary of *$125,000 for the first year, pending successful completion of the criminal check.
Board Member: I second the motion.
Vote by roll call.

CALL CANDIDATE AND OFFER POSITION AS THE MOTION READS (B)

If candidate accepts, the following motion is to be made:
Board Member: I hereby make a motion that we employ _____
as the new superintendent of Home Town Community Schools for a contract period of three years, at a base salary of $125,000 for the first year, pending successful completion of the criminal check.
Board Member: I second the motion.

Vote by roll call.

*As previously approved and published

May 12, 20__

Sally Smitty
654 Forest Trails
Everywhere, IL 87654

Dear Sally,

At a meeting of the Home Town Community Schools Board of Education held on May 12, 20__, _____, Assistant Superintendent for the ABC School District in Blue Sky, Michigan, was appointed to the position of superintendent for the Home Town Community Schools.

On behalf of the Home Town Board of Education, I would like to take this opportunity to thank you for the courtesy of your interview.

The Board and I sincerely appreciated your interest in the Home Town Community Schools, and we wish you much success as you pursue your search for a superintendent position.

Sincerely,

Consultant's Signature

Reference # 38

May 12, 200_

Jim Jolly
987 High Trail
Boomtown, IN 67823

Dear Jim,

At a meeting of the Home Town Community Schools Board of Education held on May 12, 200_, _____, Assistant Superintendent for the ABC School District in Blue Sky, Michigan, was appointed to the position of superintendent for the Home Town Community Schools.

On behalf of the Home Town Board of Education, I would like to take this opportunity to thank you for the courtesy of your interview and the hospitality shown the site visit team.

The Board and I sincerely appreciated your interest in the Home Town Community Schools, and we wish you much success as you pursue your search for a superintendent position.

Sincerely,

Consultant's Signature

Reference # 39

To: All Home Town Community Schools Employees and Citizens
From: Consultant name
Re: Superintendent Appointment
Date: May 12, 20__

The Home Town Community Schools Board of Education, at a special board meeting held on May 11, 2006, heard reports from team members who visited the work places of superintendent candidates _____ and _____. After the report and discussion, the board voted to offer _____, Assistant Superintendent for the ABC School District in Blue Sky, Michigan, the position of superintendent of the Home Town Community Schools.

Dr. _____ has accepted the position and plans to begin her new duties on July 1, 20__.

I would like to take this opportunity to thank each and every one of you for the extra time and effort you put forth in giving your input to the Board of Education in this most important decision. I know the Board appreciated and valued your opinions and interest.

It was a pleasure to work with you, and I wish you well as you guide the Home Town Community Schools and the entire community forward in the twenty-first century.